Queering
the Text

Other books by Andrew Ramer
little pictures
Angel Answers
Revelations for a New Millennium
Two Flutes Playing

(with Donna Cunningham)
The Spiritual Dimensions of Healing Addictions
Further Dimensions of Healing Addictions

(with Alma Daniel and Timothy Wyllie)
Ask Your Angels

Queering the Text

Biblical, Medieval, and Modern Jewish Stories

Andrew Ramer

Foreword by
Jay Michaelson
Afterword by
Rabbi Camille Shira Angel *and*
Rabbi Dev Noily

RESOURCE *Publications* • Eugene, Oregon

Resource Publications
A division of Wipf and Stock Publishers
199 W 8th Ave, Suite 3
Eugene, OR 97401

Queering the Text
Biblical, Medieval, and Modern Jewish Stories
By Ramer, Andrew
Copyright© by Ramer, Andrew
ISBN 13: 978-1-5326-6512-7

Publication date 2/18/2020
Previously published by Lethe Press,

Preface to the 2020 Reprint Edition

I grew up in a world of stories, and it's in stories that I find myself, know myself, and know the world. I remember the very first stories I learned in Hebrew School, about Adam and Eve, the Flood, and my favorite ones: about Abraham and his father Terah, an idol maker. How stunned and sadden I was when we first began to read the Torah itself and I discovered that my favorite stories weren't in it! But those stories about stories—*midrashim*—fed me all those years ago and still feed me. And as a gay Jewish man, it was the absence of stories about myself, about women, and about other queer people that inspired me to write this book, wanting to add back into our long tradition some of what's been missing.

I like to call the genre I write in "Queer Feminist Speculative-Fiction Theology," and that's what you'll find here—stories that I wish I'd grown up hearing, that you may have wished you'd heard too. There are lesbian stories here, there are bi and trans stories, but this book was written by a man who loves men; in fact, the middle section is entirely a series of such stories. It was only after the book was first published that I realized that, between the biblical and medieval sections, I should have included a section of stories about Jewish lesbians reading Sappho in ancient Alexandria. Regret can be a marvelous muse.

This book is the first of four volumes of *midrash*, and I use that word in the broadest sense possible. In the next book, *Torah Told Different,* I included a story in the fourth section, "The Five Books of Motion," that's called "Alexandria—The Hidden Text," which is about just such ancient women loving women. The book after that one, *Deathless,* is a fictional autobiography of one of our lesbian ancestors, and the inspiration for the final book, *Fragments of the Brooklyn Talmud,* came from daydreams I was having about a lesbian rabbi living in Brooklyn eighty years from now.

I'm grateful to come from and to live in a tradition in which we tell and retell stories. My idea of heaven is for all of us to sit together around a vast feasting table at an endless Passover Seder, an endless feast of words. My hope as you read these stories is that they will fill in certain gaps in our history and awaken in you your own stories, from your past, for our present, and to feed the rippling strands of our unfolding future.

Foreword

~: Jay Michaelson :~

Foreword :~

My guess is that most readers of this book will be lesbian, gay, bisexual, or transgendered — some of the many sexual and gender identities now subsumed under the reclaimed label of "queer." It's only natural: like seeks out like, especially when, as Andrew Ramer says in his introduction, "like" is so hard to find in a library with so many erasures and gaps.

But *Queering the Text* makes a case for a broader readership. These contemporary *midrashim* — on texts from the Bible, the "Golden Age" of Spain, and other strands of Jewish tradition — show that when a previously marginalized group transforms tradition, it transforms it for everybody. None of us — gay, straight or the rest of us; male, female, or the rest of us — emerges from these re-readings the same as we entered them. This is the gift of queer voices like Ramer's — not that they petition to be let into a normal Jewish world, but, like the feminist pioneers of the last several decades, they assert: we are here, we deserve to be here, and we are going to change things.

In its imaginary (knowing Andrew as I do, perhaps the right word is "visionary") renderings of Biblical, medieval, and contemporary queer Jews, this book doesn't merely insert a lesbian prophetess or gay patriarch into a preexisting Biblical text. Like the best of midrash, it transforms the text itself. Rather like Anita Diamant's *The Red Tent*, *Queering the Text* presents us with a God/dess who transforms genders, a Biblical Israelite religion in close intercourse with Canaanite and other polytheisms, and an entire suppressed history of same-sex love that dates back to the primordial generations and is remembered and recounted by subsequent ones.

In other words, this is queering the text – not merely imagining queers in the text, or providing a queer reading of text, or some other innocuous literary procedure. The text itself changes, and we do as a result. While this may seem radical, it is, in fact, part of a longstanding anti-fundamentalist strand of the Jewish tradition, which sees the Bible not as a quasi-historical record with a single correct interpretation, but a font of multiple interpretations. Plurality of meanings and conflicting interpretations are not a sign of the text's or our weakness – they are a sign of its strength.

That said, the transformations Ramer proposes may in fact bring us closer to the "original meanings" (whatever that means) of the Biblical texts themselves. Biblical scholar Ken Stone has suggested that the sexual distinctions the elites of Israel sought to impose upon the nation were meant to demarcate national distinctions as well – the binary opposition between 'Israelite' and 'Canaanite' being more rhetorical than real. We don't do what they do, the Law seems to say, and thus We aren't Them. Ramer picks up where Stone leaves off, imagining a far more porous Israel than that presented in Scripture, and one richer and more varied in its expression of Divinity. Here are Naamah and Nogah, Bezalel and Oholiab, Deborah and

Foreword :~

Yael; here are sacred prostitutes and holy eunuchs; and here is a world in which what Stone astutely describes as elite Israelite "border anxiety" is transformed into a popular border-crossing delight.

Likewise in the later portions of *Queering the Text*, which bring us to the multicultural Sepharad and to our contemporary day. It was likely in imitation of their Muslim colleagues that medieval (male) Jewish poets composed homoerotic love poems to young men. Ramer takes things a step further, venturing beyond literary convention to imagine a host of intra- and inter-generational loves, rendered in prose and verse. Here again, the lines crossed are not merely those of sexuality; Ramer's lusty medievalists are commanded to transgress the law, impelled to rebel, and inspired, by sacred lust, to bridge the gaps between sexual and spiritual.

Arriving in the present day in the third section, with UPS, HIV, and Ph.D's in tow, is at first something of a shock: our own moment can seem small in comparison with the narratives of older times. But for many readers, I suspect, the last tales in this volume contain Ramer's most radical proposal of all. For here, not only does queer experience reshape the Bible, but, Ramer daringly suggests, the Bible can productively shape queer experience. For queer readers whose only contact with religious tradition has been exclusion and marginalization, the crossing of this particular boundary may seem like too much of an encroachment. But this, too, is the challenge Ramer issues: to reclaim the tradition is to allow it access to our own intimacies as well.

Do Ramer's hidden traditions – *Queering the Text* ends by imagining an entire parallel line of non-Biblical

Hebrews — actually exist? And if they do not, is it necessary to invent them? Maybe only the angels know for sure. Then again, if anyone's in touch with those watchers and keepers of secret tradition, it surely is Andrew Ramer, prophet and poet and heretical preacher all wrapped up in one.

Let me end with a confession. Many times, I wanted to take *Queering the Text* and bash it over the head of every reactionary rabbi I know. Amidst the batteries I would shout, "See! This is what can happen when the religious spirit is liberated! This is what would result if our souls were encouraged to dance!" Unfortunately, this volume is too slim to do much damage in such a brute, physical way. I therefore hand it to you, so that it may work its far more insidious magic on your heart.

∼: Table of Contents :∼

Preface to the 2020 Reprint Edition ∼: iii

Foreword ∼: v
  Jay Michaelson

Introduction ∼: xv

Part One
The Genizah of Dreams: 22 *Midrashim* ∼: 1

Part Two
Al-Andalus: *Tales of an Imaginary Spain* ∼: 73
  Remembering Spain ∼: 75
  Reading "Shemot" ∼: 79
  In Granada ∼: 83
  The Rabbi and the Court Physician ∼: 87
  Erev Shabbat ∼: 93
  Before Arvit ∼: 97
  The Vizier ∼: 101
  In the Marketplace ∼: 107
  The Hidden Mirror ∼: 111
  Before there was Law ∼: 117
  My Forsaken Garden ∼: 119
  The Christian ∼: 121
  The Commandments ∼: 125
  Twice a Heretic ∼: 129
  Toledo in Winter ∼: 135
  The Tutor ∼: 137
  The Dreamer and the Dream ∼: 141

The Street of Butchers	~: 145
While Praying	~: 149
The Rabbi's Dilemma	~: 153
In the Domed Hall	~: 157
Before the Expulsion	~: 163

Part Three
Avodah: *Divine Service* ~: 171
  Shacharit: Light in the Tree ~: 173
  Musaf: Pink Izzy ~: 189
  Mincha: Gazing out of a Window ~: 205
  Ma'ariv: The Return of the Hebrew Bedouin ~: 221

Afterword ~: 241
  Rabbi Camille Shira Angel and Rabbi Dev Noily

This book is dedicated to the queer youth of the future, hoping that they will always know, with all their heart, all their soul, and all their might, that they belong to the Family of Eve and the House of Israel, the God-Wrestler.

Introduction

Introduction :~

Judaism is a text-based tradition. From the time of the Bible until the present we who the *Qur'an* calls "People of the Book" have expressed ourselves in words. Sadly, tragically, for women and queer people, until recently there have been few textual mirrors for our lives in any of our sacred or scholarly books. But that is changing, and this book is a part of the transformation, the recognition, of who we are and how we fit into the Jewish world.

There are three sections in this book. The first plays with texts from the Hebrew Bible, the second was inspired by homoerotic poems written in medieval Spain, and the stories in the third section are set in the present and play with the Bible and other texts. For me this book is a work of *Tikkun Olam*, a sacred work of Cosmic Repair. I wrote it with the hope that other queer people of faith won't have to wander in the wilderness for forty years as I did, looking for their spiritual home in our tradition. My fondest wish is that these tales will add to the conversation that Jews and non-Jews, queer and non-queer people are having, about inclusion, diversity, and human freedom. The Bible, in the book of Genesis, tells us that we were created in the image of God. That verse of text is the foundation for all of these stories.

~: Part One :~
The Genizah of Dreams: 22 Midrashim

In the Jewish tradition sacred books are not discarded or destroyed when they're too old and ragged to use. Instead they're deposited in a storeroom called a *genizah*. A genizah, which means "hiding place" in Hebrew, is also the repository for books considered heretical, but which contain the sacred name of God and therefore can't be destroyed either. The most famous genizah was discovered in 1890 during the renovation of the Ben Ezra Synagogue in Fostat, Old Cairo, built in 882. The hundreds of thousands of pages found there, most of them written between the 11th and 13th centuries, vastly increased our knowledge of medieval Jewish life. It's also possible that the Dead Sea Scrolls were part of an ancient genizah, stored away because they were worn out.

I have called this section a Genizah of Dreams for two reasons. First because the "documents" it includes are "heretical" in that they are all "queer," non-normative, questioning the un-queer thrust of most Jewish texts. And second, because the stories you will find here are the kinds of tales I wished I had discovered as a young gay man, struggling to find a place for myself in Judaism. They are documents from a parallel reality, retrieved from hidden shelves in the deepest recesses of my heart and my mind. They express what is most sacred to me – the ability to be true to one's soul, and the capacity to love ourselves and others in alignment with the calling of our soul.

In Hebrew, these stories are called *midrashim*, from the root *drash*, "to inquire." Midrashim are designed to fill gaps in scripture. For example, the Torah prohibits work on the Sabbath, without defining what's forbidden. Legal midrashim enumerate the categories of banned work. Narrative midrashim expand or interpret biblical stories, as in the tales of Adam's first wife Lilith, who isn't mentioned in the Torah. The earliest preserved midrashim date back to the first two centuries of the Common Era.

Just as medieval European artists painted Biblical characters in garments they wore themselves, the rabbis of old crafted midrashim in which the women and men of the Bible were seen as their own contemporaries. For instance, there are tales of Jacob studying Torah with his father Isaac (even though the Torah wouldn't be given till generations later), as if they were students in a talmudic academy that only existed centuries after that. We queer readers of Torah can do the same thing, by telling stories that are relevant to own time and our own concerns, which will reframe our sacred texts in ways its authors might not have understood – or accepted – just as the rabbis of old did with their midrashim.

Our Bible is the product of many revisions, and I believe that there were once other torahs, torahs that may have embraced what we now call queerness. For example, *kedeshim*, a Hebrew word that used to be translated as "sodomites," and is usually now interpreted as "cultic male prostitutes," derives from the root word for holiness. What does this tell us about the behavior and beliefs of some of our ancestors?

My stories are told in a number of different styles, from mock-scriptural to modern narrative. None of them are legal, although I address the two verses in *Leviticus* about men having sex with other men in the story "The Holy One." I haven't dealt with some passages that are open to queer interpretations, like the account of Ham uncovering his father Noah's nakedness, or the one about Lot and the men of Sodom.

There are twenty-two stories in my collection, one for each letter of the Hebrew alphabet. Most of my tales begin with the passage of scripture that inspired them, although in a few cases lines from the Bible are woven into the stories. The quoted passages all come the Jewish Publication Society translation of the Bible, *Tanakh: The Holy Scriptures*, but each time God's name appears I have replaced the substitution "The Lord" with YHWH, the English equivalent of the Hebrew letters of that sacred name.

~: Part Two :~
Al Andalus: Tales of an Imaginary Spain

Some writers need roots, lineage, ancestry; like tree from acorn, linked back, emergent. For me, 20th and 21st century creature, cognizant of the Torah's prohibitions on men being with men, and conscious always of the absence of queer stories in our sacred texts – where can I turn but to medieval Spain? There, and nowhere else we know about in Jewish history until the present, rabbis, sages, and scholars wrote words of love to other men. We know these writers, from what is called the Golden Age in Spain: Samuel HaNagid, Moses ibn Ezra, Solomon ibn Gabirol, and Judah HaLevi. Their poems were almost always written to young men, and most scholars believe that in writing as they did those poets were only following the Arabic literary convention of the time. They also assume that the "boys," the "cupbearers," "fawns," and "gazelles" in those poems, were always Muslim, but I don't. In

Introduction :~

my imaginary Spain, famous rabbis were writing real love poems to real young men, most of whom were Jewish.

Very few Jews know about these poets, and we have no idea of how their work might have influenced our lives if the Muslim Spain that was their home hadn't been reconquered by Catholic Spaniards, who expelled the Jews in 1492. To give you a feel for what those men were writing, I quote a short poem by Samuel HaNagid. He lived from 953 to 1056 and was the vizier to the Muslim king of Granada in addition to being the head of the Spanish Jewish community. This translation is by Jerome Rothenberg and Harris Lenowitz. It's one of the first of these poems that I came across, and it remains one of my favorites. The word *yod* is the name of the smallest letter of the Hebrew alphabet, almost like a floating comma, which is also the first letter of God's sacred four-letter name, often translated as Yahweh.

> *I'd sell my soul for that fawn*
> *of a boy nightwalker*
> *to the sound of 'ud and flute playing*
> *who saw the glass in my hand and said*
> *"drink the wine from between my lips"*
> *and the moon was a* yod *drawn on*
> *the cover of dawn – in gold ink...*

After reading that first poem I hunted for others. They are tucked away in other places, including anthologies by Raymond Scheindlin and Peter Cole. Last year I had the pleasure of hearing Cole read at the Jewish Community Library in San Francisco. After the reading, while he was signing books, I asked him if the tradition of men writing poems to and about other men had stopped with the Expulsion. He said no, that recently in an archive, in Albania I think he said, similar poems from a later day were discovered, all as yet untranslated. Did those Sephardic poets know that a day would come when men who love men, Jewish men who love men, would walk together hand in hand, form gay synagogues, become ordained as rabbis, and write queer prayers? Did they have the conversations we have, about Jewish law and their place in the Jewish world? And did they love other men with an inner freedom we still lack? Even if they didn't, they and their poems make us possible, even if we haven't known their words or heard their names, and even if they never imagined us, or needed us, in order for them to love in their own ways.

So Spain, yes. Muslim Spain. Jewish Spain. Sephardic ribald passionate man-loving Spain. In linked, inter-woven stories, written from my New Spain, San Francisco, California, former Spanish Catholic colony, where I sit and study and write my evocations. In these stories it's not my intention to recreate the Spain that existed from the tenth to twelfth centuries under Muslim rule until the expulsion of the Jews in 1492 by the Catholic rulers of a newly reunified country. My Spain is one of inference and shadow, of reference and allusion, as true but no more real than Cavafy's Hellenistic world, or Gilbert and Sullivan's Japan in *The Mikado*. My tales are like Whitman's, who dreamt of parallel realities and immanent futures that still stand eagerly on thresholds and linger in doorways, as the dominant culture debates or avoids debating the civil rights and sanctity of same-sex marriage.

Introduction ≻

Hebrew love poetry often refers back to *Song of Songs* in the Bible. On the surface it's a collection of erotic heterosexual love poems, mostly written in women's voices, although Paul Johnson, in his book *The Song of Songs: A Gay Love Poem?*, claims that it was originally written by one man to another. Tradition ascribes its authorship to King Solomon. Due to its subject matter it was one of the last books to be admitted to the canon, and then only because it came to be seen as an allegory of the love between God and Israel. Rabbi Akiva said of it, "All scripture is sacred, but 'Song of Songs' is the Holy of Holies." My Andalusian muses wrote with *Song of Songs* in their minds, and it's influenced my work as well. The stories at the heart of the book are all about men who love men, reflecting the deepest dreams of my own heart.

~: Part Three :~
Avodah: Divine Service

There are four longer stories in the final section of the book. The title of this section was initially inspired by a verse in the Talmud, from a section called *Pirke Avot – Chapters of the Fathers*, which reads, "The world stands on three things, Torah, divine service, and acts of loving kindness." This book is grounded in Torah. My hope is that its publication will be seen as an act of loving kindness. And the stories in the third section, *Avodah* – Divine Service, are named for the four traditional synagogue services offered on Shabbat: *shacharit* – the morning service, *musaf* – the additional service, *minchah* – the afternoon service, and *ma'ariv* – the evening service.

These four stories all take place in the present, or in *a* present. Biblical prohibitions against male same-sex love have warped the lives of hundreds of generations of Jews and countless others across the globe who have been influenced by the Jewish Bible. Rabbinical Judaism carried on and extended those prohibitions, by including women in its list of prohibitions, and verses about cross-dressing and rigid binary gender notions shape our lives to this day. Fortunately, in this time, rabbinic texts about multiple genders and other queer concerns that I was never taught in Hebrew School are being read, studied, and written about, texts that few have had access to for hundreds of years.

Over the last decades, the writings of feminist Jews, and the recrafting of Jewish ritual life to include women rabbis, female God language, women's Seders and other women-centered rituals, has not threatened the sanctity of Jewish life, but enhanced it. And it is my hope that the stories in this book will do the same, in their own small way – helping to redefine and enhance Jewish life for all queer people, lesbian, gay, bisexual, intersexed, and transgendered. So my characters in Part Three move through a landscape that is transformed, but not fundamentally alien. And I hope that as you wander through it you will find yourself there too, whether you are queer or not.

Andrew Ramer / Ayal Shabtai ben Gita v'Yaakov
May 2009 / Iyar 5769

Introduction ∾

Love your neighbor as yourself. Leviticus 19:18

The stone that the builders rejected has become the chief cornerstone. Psalm 118:22

Re-vision – the act of look back, of seeing with fresh eyes, of entering an old text from a new critical direction – is for women more than a chapter in cultural history: it is an act of survival. Adrienne Rich

The Genizah *of* Dreams

~: 22 Midrashim :~

The Genizah of Dreams :~

~: Without a Beginning א :~

In the beginning God created the heaven and the earth.
>No time. No space. And therefore, no beginning.

Now the earth was unformed and void, and darkness was upon the face of the deep.
>Only light, light, light. Ever-present and eternal.

And the spirit of God hovered over the face of the waters.
>And the light was God. And the light is God. And the light will always be God.

And God said: "Let there be light." And there was light.
>And from Her body, which is light, God births all that is; galaxies, stars, worlds.

And God saw the light, that it was good.
>With no separation between Her, Her body, and all that She has given birth to.

And God divided the light from the darkness.
>And the oneness of all that is, She breathes with it and calls it Good.

And God called the light Day. And the darkness He called Night.
> And the Goodness breathes with Her; galaxies, stars, worlds.

And there was evening and there was morning, one day.
> And there is one day only, always; radiant, joyful, and never ending.

Genesis 1:1-5

The Genizah of Dreams :~

~: Let There Be Life ב :~

And God said, "Let us make man in our image, after our likeness. They shall rule the fish of the sea, the birds of the sky, the cattle, the whole earth, and all the creeping things that creep upon the earth." And He created man in His image, in the image of God He created him; male and female created He them.   Genesis 1:26-27

After God had given birth to all the worlds, joyful and radiant, It breathed the breath of life into Its creation. With that breath It birthed angels and archangels, seraphim, cherubim, and all forms of embodied life. It birthed beings that swim and slither, that fly and crawl, that walk and wiggle, and beings that don't move at all.

God blessed them and God said to them: "Be fertile and increase, fill the earth and master it; and rule the fish of the sea, the birds of the sky, and all the living things that creep on earth."   Genesis 1:28

And all the life that It birthed was connected in a vast web, body to body and soul to soul. And out through that web It breathed the truth of Its creation – that all who remember the web will prosper, and all who forget it will struggle, struggle in ways that are of their own making. It breathed out this truth to worlds with one gender and worlds with two genders. It breathed out this truth to worlds with many genders and worlds with no genders. It breathed out this truth to worlds with constant genders and to worlds with changeable genders. God, the Source of Life, breathed the truth of Its creation out to every part of it.

The Genizah of Dreams :~

~: The Seeker ג :~

And the days of Adam after he begat Seth were eight hundred years; and he begat sons and daughters. And all the days that Adam lived were nine hundred and thirty years; and he died. Genesis 5:4-5

Jerah was the youngest son of Eve and Adam. Even as a boy he knew that he was different from his many brothers and their sons and from the sons of his many sisters. When he was older he set out to find someone else who was like him. He walked and wandered from village to village and town to town, to all the places where they had settled, but nowhere did he meet anyone who was like him. Weary, after months of wandering, he came to the village of his favorite sister, Hodesh.

Now Hodesh had a son named Naam, and Naam was the same age as Jerah. When Jerah and Naam looked at each other for the first time, their hearts like birds flew out of their breasts toward each other.

And their lips called out the other's true name. And their bodies opened, one to the other, so that their souls could dance joyfully together on the earth.

Jerah and Naam built for themselves a house of stone in the village established by Hodesh. They lived there happily for seven hundred and twenty-eight years, in midst of their family. And they were buried side by side in the cave where first they had buried Hodesh.

~: The Makers of Beauty ⁊ :~

Lamech took himself two wives: the name of the one was Adah, and the name of the other was Zillah. Adah bore Jabal: he was the ancestor of those who dwell in tents and amidst herds. And the name of his brother was Jubal: he was the ancestor of all who play the lyre and the pipe. As for Zillah, she bore Tubal-cain, who forged all implements of copper and iron. And the sister of Tubal-cain was Naamah.   Genesis 4:17-22

Naamah was the ancestor of all those who create beautiful things. With wool from the flocks of Jabal, Naamah and her beloved Nogah the daughter of Inanna, spun fiber and wove it into fabric. They made garments and carrying pouches, they made hangings and carpets. They mixed berries, leaves, stems, roots, and ground stones to make dyes. With their dyes they colored the fibers they had spun and wove them into beautiful patterns.

Next they mixed plants and ground stones, they mixed them with water and oil and they made paint for the very first time. Before that time no one had ever yet painted on stone or on animal skins, on wood or cloth, or even painted their own bodies. But Naamah, she did these things, she did them for the first time. She and her beloved Nogah, together they did all these things. With tools made by Naamah's brother Tubal-cain, Nogah and Naamah carved wood and stone, they carved bone and ivory. They carved circles and spirals, they carved flowers and animals, they carved birds and rivers, mountains and trees. All that they carved and made was beautiful.

And all the beauty that they made, they made it as an offering to the Mother of us all. And She saw what they had made, and She smiled with pleasure and told them that everything they made was good, yes, it was very good.

~: The Messenger ה :~

Jacob was left alone. And a man wrestled with him until the break of dawn.   Genesis 32:23-25
Said he, "Your name shall no longer be Jacob, but Israel, for you have striven with beings divine and human and you have prevailed." Jacob asked, "Pray tell me your name." But he said, "You must not ask my name!" And he took leave of him there. So Jacob named the place Peniel, meaning, "I have seen a divine being face to face, yet my life has been preserved."   Genesis 32:29-31

It was a moonless night. The sky was strewn with stars. I built myself a small fire. It cast a tiny flickering pool of light around me that quickly vanished in the darkness.

I didn't see him; nor did I hear him approach. Suddenly he was standing across the fire from me, hands on his hips, looking down at me as I sat on the hard dry earth. The wood was crackling. The air was cold. His face was dark and expressionless, but he was staring at me as if he knew me.

"Peace be to you," I said to him. He said nothing back, just stepped closer. It was only then that I saw his wings. They were vast, like the fringed shawl of a holy one, dark, dark as his skin, dark as the night that births new mornings. He opened them wide and stepped over the fire. I stood, my legs shaking.

My heart was beating furiously. I was sure that he could hear it in the silence. I wanted to run but I was frozen in that spot. He stepped close, reached out and placed his hands on my shoulders. And he looked down into my eyes as if they were two wells empty of water, till his gaze had penetrated to my very heart, filling it to overflowing. Then he opened his wings, further than I would have thought possible, and wrapped them around me, pulling me closer. And he wrapped his arms around my back, so that my chest was pressed flat against his chest. And I felt myself vanishing in his embrace, like a stream that washes into a river, as we stood chest to chest, belly to belly, thigh to thigh.

He leaned down and kissed me. I opened my lips to him. And so it was, all night, that the two of us grappled on the ground, a man and an angel, his wings and his arms wrapped around me. We battled and made love till the sky began to lighten, when he pressed me to the earth and entered me. Wrenched apart and then pushed into bliss, he filled me with light. Then, bathed in the waters of my flesh, we curled together by the remains of the fire, breathing softly together.

I asked him his name. He would not tell me. I asked him for a blessing. He said, with a grin, "Wasn't this blessing enough for you?" I looked away, ashamed, for he was right. But he lifted my chin with his hands, smiling. Then he kissed me again. I stroked his back, feeling the way that his wings grew out of it. I caressed his face, looked him deep in those dark dark eyes again. Then my arms were empty and he was gone, just as suddenly as he had appeared. And I was alone again.

The Genizah of Dreams :~

~: The Cave of Pleasure 1 :~

Now Dinah, the daughter whom Leah had borne to Jacob, went out to visit the daughters of the land.

Genesis 34:1-2

Fourteen year old Dinah and her little sisters Rizpah and Hadar were crossing the stream that separated their father's grazing land from that of the local chieftain Hamor, land that Jacob had purchased from Hamor for one hundred *kesitahs*.

Sandals in hand, holding the bottom of their robes up, the sisters were slipping and sliding on wet stones, laughing as they made their way across. Rizpah and Hadar dashed ahead, laughing, as Dinah followed. As she made her way across the stream, Dinah was thinking about a hand-clapping song that Hamor's daughter Katirat taught her on her last visit, about the goddess Asherah. "Oh, she is a mighty tree," the song began. "She is a tree of life that reaches from earth to heaven." One clap, four claps, two claps. She kept repeating it in her mind till she reached the other side, where she dried off her feet and slipped into her sandals.

The closer Dinah and her sisters got to the town, the more her heart swelled with thoughts of Katirat. The two of them began their friendship by singing and dancing together with all the village girls. Now that she was older, Dinah wanted to be alone with her new friend. Her heart beat faster as she approached the town, its stone walls glowing in the sunlight. And there was Katirat, waiting for her by the open gate. "Come with me," she said to Dinah, as her sisters darted through the gate to meet their friends.

Katirat led Dinah around the town walls. At first they walked and then they ran, toward a cave that Katirat wanted to show her. It was dark inside, but Dinah wasn't afraid. She was with her friend now. Out of breath, the two stood in the darkness. Neither of them spoke. And then Dinah began to sing a song that she learned from Leah her mother, a song of her own people that she wanted to teach her friend. "Asherah, the Lady of the Sea, she opened her body to Tallai, the Lady of Rain. And oh, how Tallai came to her, wet and beautiful."

There were more verses to the song, but suddenly Dinah's throat was clogged. She couldn't find her voice. All that she could do was reach out a trembling hand, and place it on Katirat's warm shoulder. And the two were wrapped fast in each other's arms, their young breasts pressed together. And their hands began to travel on each other's backs, thighs, faces, bellies, pressing over cloth, seeking and hungering for flesh, in the darkness of the cave, at the north of Hamor's village. And soon they lowered themselves to the dark earth, like ocean, like rain, becoming the two goddesses.

"And Tallai the Lady of the Rain, she poured herself into the body of Asherah, the Lady of the Sea. And the two waters met, dark and shining."

The Genizah of Dreams :~

~: On Bended Knee ⸙ :~

When Joseph was taken down to Egypt, a certain Egyptian, Potiphar, a courtier of Pharaoh and his chief steward, bought him from the Ishmaelites who had brought him there.   Genesis 39:1
Now Joseph was well built and handsome. Genesis 39:6

God of the Hebrews, I am an Egyptian, but please accept my offering and hear my prayer. I have made offerings to my own gods, but they do not hear me. The Hebrew who I bought in the marketplace is torturing me. I come to you on my knees to beg you to make him take notice of me. I could take him. I know that. He is powerless beside me. I own him. But what kind of a man would that make me? No, that isn't how I want him. That isn't what I want. I want his spirit, I want his soul, I want him to love me.

That day in the market! It was hot. I was looking to purchase a new boy but there was nothing in the merchandise that I liked. I was about to leave when I noticed him, standing in the back of a cluster of other youths. They all looked so dejected, while he stood, so tall, so proud, so beautiful. I had to buy him, and now I have turned over my entire household to him, something I never did with any of my Egyptian stewards. I have given all of this to him, a Hebrew, a hairy nomad, dust covered and wild. Although I made him shave his beard. His cheeks are smooth now. And his eyes! Green like the sea in a face so dark. And his lips, made for kissing. Made for kissing – me! But does he see me? No. Does he smile at me? No. His smiles are the smiles of a slave for his master. But I want him to smile at me as a man smiles at another man, smile at me the way that I smile at him, with desire. I want him to want me, to reach out to me, to be lover and master of me as he has become the master of my heart.

O, god of the Hebrews, now I see my wife looking at him, yearning for him. He looks at her just as he looks at me. But what if that changes? It would kill me if he gave himself to her when he refuses to give himself to me. I tremble when he walks past me. I shake when he hands me something. I am a man of power and position. I own him. But when he is around I sigh and look away like a boy of twelve. Please hear me. I will give you the best of my flocks and my fields. Your people will be well fed because of me. So why do you curse me? Why have you sent me this Joseph of yours to drive me crazy?

His smell, as fragrant as the incense I just offered you. And the shape of his head, and the line of his shoulders when he turns away from me. They're like daggers of copper in my heart. If he should favor my wife, I would send him out of my house. I might kill him. When all that I want to do is touch him, love him, and be loved by him. So hear my prayer. Accept my offering. And bend his heart toward me, god of his own people. I am humble before you. I am weak. I am Potiphar, the Egyptian, groveling.

The Genizah of Dreams :~

~: Healing Hands ת :~

The King of Egypt spoke to the Hebrew midwives, one of whom was named Shifrah, the other Puah."

Exodus 1:15

Just before dawn they were awakened by Jahmai, whose wife Haggith had gone into labor, almost a month early. Puah grabbed her staff, her bundle of herbs, and ran after him, just as the first light of morning painted a coral streak across the dark sky. And then later, as Shifrah squatted in front of their mud brick hut, bent over a tiny fire, stirring her morning meal of fish and grains, little Miriam came running. "My mother is calling for you." Removing the clay pot from the fire and putting it out with sand, Shifrah gathered up her own medicine bag and followed Miriam to her family's hut.

This was Haggith's first child. Her labor was long and difficult. For a time Puah thought that neither mother nor baby would make it. The sun had cleared the top of the sky and was sinking when at last Haggith's baby entered the world, tiny, and feet first. But she was a strong little girl, with strong lungs, and as night fell, a happy, weary Puah made her way home.

Jochebed's labor was different. The mother of several children already, she was smiling as Shifrah entered her hut. She knew what she was doing, but welcomed the comforting presence of the woman who had been with her when Aaron, Miriam, Itai, and Peninnah had been born. Squatting behind her, massaging her belly, Shifrah held and supported Jochebed as waves of contraction came and went. Her baby, a little boy with curly dark hair, entered the world quietly and easily. Mother and newborn washed, the hut cleaned, the rest of the family welcomed in to meet the baby, Shifrah slipped out and quietly made her way home.

Puah returned to find Shifrah bent over a new fire, stirring onions and fennel into a pot that contained that morning's leftovers. They ate sitting in front of their hut, and quietly told each other about the new children they had welcomed into the world. And then later, on the mattress of grasses that they shared, wrapped in each other's arms, they whispered together words of thankful prayer to Shaddai, for allowing them to be witnesses to the miracle of new life. And then they rode the waves of that miracle as it washed between them, the midwives of the Hebrews.

The Genizah of Dreams :~

~: The Tent of Miriam ۷ :~

Then Miriam the prophetess, Aaron's sister, took a timbrel in her hand, and all the women went out after her in dance with timbrels.   Exodus 15:20

The sea was wide and cold. The water was waist high in some places, shoulder high and swift in others. Tibni lost the small bundle of things he'd hurried to gather before they left. It was carried away in the current. Miriam watched him struggle after it and called out, "Let it go, cousin. Keep walking." Iscah stumbled, and her little daughter Elat, clinging to her back, was nearly swept away. But Shifra grabbed the child and saved her. And they all pushed on, panting and cold, following the path that Moses had charted.

From the back of the line Miriam saw her brother Moses grasp at reeds on the opposite shore, and then pull himself up on the bank. Aaron and his children were right behind him, then the rest of our tiny clan climbed out of the water and stepped into freedom. And gasping, coughing up water, muddy and dripping, alone, in groups, hand in hand, the rest of her people pushed and pulled themselves up on the far side of the sea. Lastly Miriam and her beloved Zahavah, at the very end to make sure that everyone else had made it, emerged from the waters, together. And free.

Some were sobbing. Others were standing, shivering, numb and afraid. Others were wandering in the crowd, looking for their loved ones. Moses, beaming, reached down to Aaron's granddaughter Batshua and raised her high up over his head. Then he spun her around and the spray of water made rainbows in the morning sky.

They'd fled in secret in the middle of the night and walked for hours, fearful that they'd be followed. But the plague had killed thousands, guards and soldiers included, so no one came in pursuit – although at every step it felt as if they had. And now, now they were free!

Miriam looked at Zahavah. Zahavah knew that look. The spirit of prophecy had entered Miriam. She threw back her head and let out a long loud cry. Everyone stopped, and then, pushing their way through the crowd, all the women joined her. They had no drums. They had no timbrels. They had no sistrums or hand bells. They'd left Egypt with only the essential they could carry on their backs. But they had their hands to clap with. The midwives Puah and Shifrah led the women in a circle dance, with Miriam and Zahavah in the middle, hand in hand. Then Miriam began to sing the song of God that was moving through her. After each line the women repeated it, as they always did when she was given a holy song.

"As if the waters had parted for us."
"As if God had parted them Herself."
"We crossed. We crossed into freedom."
"Yes, the waters of the sea parted, and then we crossed."
"The waves rose up around us like horses."
"Yes, like horses with soldiers coming after us."
"But we crossed. Everyone of us crossed."
"The waters parted and then we crossed into freedom."

All the men and boys were gathered around the women as they sang and danced, clapping and cheering them on. And when the power began to ebb, when the song and dance began to slow down, Miriam let out a final cry that echoed out over the hills. Then she turned to Zahavah, in the midst of the crowd, and pulled her wet cloak over both their heads. Wrapped in each other's arms, they kissed, deeply and fully, in that tent of theirs, that first tent of freedom our people raised up in the wilderness.

The Genizah of Dreams :~

~: And They Made Sacred ᛭ :~

Now Bezalel son of Uri son of Hur of the tribe of Judah, had made all that YHWH had commanded Moses; at his side was Oholiab son of Ahisamach of the tribe of Dan. Exodus 38:22-23

The accident of meeting. Two Hebrew youths, one in service from an early age to the chief carver and metalworker in the temple of Amon-Ra, king of the Egyptian gods. The other in service to the master weaver in the temple of Isis. One day the carver sends his servant Bezalel on an errand to the temple of Isis, where the two young men see each other for the first time. And a look passes between them, a heartful look of recognition. And each remembers the other, at night on the hard dry earth in the servants' lodging in the back of the temple in which he lives and works.

Months later, after plagues and increasing hardship, word sweeps through the city that all of the

Hebrews can go free. Taking only what he can carry, Bezalel runs back to his family's tiny hut. And so too the orphaned Oholiab grabs what he can and leaves the temple of Isis, to join the rest of his people in their march to freedom. And there, in the crowd, people pushing and shoving, crying, afraid, the two see each other, smile, move toward each other. And the same look passes from eye to eye, a heartful look of soul-deep recognition. Hands find each other, hands well trained in work, but not yet in love, that say as they march from Egypt in the night, "Surely God brought us together."

In the wilderness, because of their many skills, Moses chooses the two of them to create for the people a vast portable tent and everything required to serve God. In sand, on animal skins, on shards of broken pots, they sketch out designs for ark, altar, lampstand, priestly garments, and for the great tent and enclosure that they will make, a sacred shrine to the One who in six days created the world and everything in it.

Oholiab and Bezalel train others to assist them in the work, which occupies them for months and months, in the wilderness, with limited resources. As the work progresses, from time to time they stop, catch each other's eye, and exchange a look that says, "Surely God brought us together to do this work," turning to face each other, just as the cherubim face each other, on top of the ark they make for God's holy words.

Finally, everything is complete. In a week's time Moses will dedicate the ark, altar, tabernacle, and initiate Aaron and his sons as priests. Exhausted, almost unable to believe that everything is finally done, Bezalel and Oholiab stagger toward the little stream that runs to the east of the encampment.

From months bent over a fire, hammering copper, silver, and gold, all the hair on Bezalel's arms has burned off, his skin is dry and seared. And from months bent elbow deep in large clay vats, dying blue, purple, and crimson the yarns that he and his assistants spun and wove into cloth, Oholiab's hands and arms are now a deep rich purple. That evening, as they kneel to wash beside the narrow trickling stream, lined with reeds and grasses bowing in the evening breeze, they join hands, burnt and discolored. And each says to the other, through wet palm and curled fingers, "Surely God brought us together, just like Naamah and Nogah, to create all of this beauty."

The Genizah of Dreams :~

~: The Academy of Women ב :~

His daughter was Sheerah, who built both Lower and Upper Beth-horon, and Uzzen-Shirah.

1 Chronicles 7:24

When Sheerah the granddaughter of Ephraim moved through the camp, she was tall as a date palm and her hair blew in the wind like flags on the walls of a city. Her shoulders were as broad as roof-beams made of wood from Lebanon, and her stride was as powerful as a lion's. After the people settled back in Canaan, of all the women in the Bible, we are told of no one else but Sheerah who built towns. In the hill country north of Jerusalem she built the two Beth-horons, and then she built a town she named for herself, Stronghold of Sheerah. And it was there, in Uzzen-Sheerah, that Sheerah and her beloved, Shulamit a descendant of Ishmael, created a school, a school for women who felt a calling to be teachers and healers. Women from every tribe who were lovers went there to have their unions blessed, in the names of Sheerah and Shulamit. And women from every tribe went there to study also, older teaching younger. When they completed their studies they returned home to serve the people, with sacred stories, inspired words, and with healings for body and spirit.

Generations of women studied at Sheerah's school, including three noted but unnamed elders from our past. The first was Noiyah the daughter of Yaffah, remembered as the witch of Endor who King Saul visited in his despair, begging her to summon the spirit of the prophet Samuel for him to consult with, which she did. The second was Milcah the daughter of Hamiadan, the wise woman of Tekoa who gave counsel to King David after his son Absalom had killed his half-brother Amnon for raping his sister Tamar. The third was the wise woman of Abel, Cozbi the daughter of Ahimyah, who gave counsel to David's general Joab when he was laying siege to her city. These unnamed women and their forgotten sisters, all students of Sheerah's school, were healers and far seers, able to dowse for water and bless flocks and crops. They passed their gifts on to all of their children, down through time, and many of us are awakening now to our inheritance from those women who went before us, the wise women of Israel.

The Genizah of Dreams ~

~: Tossed by Wind ל :~

In the days of Jael, caravans ceased, and wayfarers went by roundabout paths. Deliverance ceased in Israel, till you arose, O Deborah, arose, O mother in Israel.

Judges 5:6-7

"It's always been this way," Jael said to Deborah, as they stood in front of her tent, dust-covered, their hair tossed and tangled by a fierce wind blowing in from the west. "You do things your way, and I do things mine. You want me to be just like you, but I'm not, and I won't ever be."

"That's not true, my love," Deborah said, reaching out a hand to Jael, who stepped back, her hands clenched tightly behind her. "I've always honored and respected you. I've celebrated you in songs and poems. All the people of Israel know how I feel about you."

"I know that you love me, and I know that you honor me. That isn't the problem. The problem is that you want me to do things your way. And I don't. I don't want to. Your way is your way. I want you to honor mine."

"But I do!"

"No. What happened last night is a perfect example. You told me to lead a contingent of soldiers back to Hazor. But when I asked you to send someone else, you snapped at me in front of everyone and then stormed off, leaving me standing there, alone. Do you know how I felt? Do you care?"

"Jael, we're at war. Don't you understand that?"

"I understand perfectly, Deborah. But I'm not a general. I'm not a captain. I'm not a leader of troops. Why can't you understand that? You knew this about me, when we first met all those years ago at Uzzen-Sheerah. We both have different skills, and I intend to use mine in the right way, not the wrong way."

For a moment Deborah's steely composure altered. Her shoulders fell, her dark eyes went soft. "I'm sorry, my love. You're right." She expected Jael to shift as well, to soften, to take her outstretched hand. But Jael did not. Instead she sighed, pulled her hair back from her face, and gazed into the hazy distance, toward the distant sea.

"Deborah, this isn't the first time we've been through this. We discussed it in Ramah, and at your camp. I don't have it in me to go through it again. I need to go back to my camp. I have a deep sense that God wants me back there. And not just because of us, because of you. I'm not saying that things are over with us. I just need a break. So trust me. And trust yourself. All of our people are depending on you now. So please, do what you do so well, and let me go back now to find my own path."

With tears in her eyes, Deborah bowed to her beloved and turned away. The wind whipped her cloak, her robe. Ten paces away she turned and saw Jael striding off toward her horse, the wind whipping through her dark hair, and through the horse's dark mane.

The Genizah of Dreams :~

~: An Altar in the Sand מ :~

Thus Naomi returned from the country of Moab: she returned with her daughter-in-law Ruth the Moabite. They arrived in Bethlehem at the beginning of the barley harvest.   Ruth 1:22

Ruth was out in the fields, gleaning among the grains, for herself and her mother-in-law. Each day she visited someone else's fields, and Naomi knew that today she would be walking a long distance and be gone a long time. At the edge of the city Naomi took a goat path away from the fields toward the hills. There, at a distance, in a hollow, where no one could see her, she built a small altar of stones, she built it to Shaddai, the god of her people. Then she gathered kindling and struck stone to make a fire. Too poor to offer up even a single turtledove, she knelt before the altar and offered up her prayer instead.

"Shaddai, Breasted One, You who nurture and feed, who have sustained me and my beloved Ruth, come to me now. You know her. She is a stubborn woman. I tried to make her turn back to stay with her own people. But she clung to me, she refused. She joined herself to me, and to Your people. And the time that we have had together is most beautiful to me. Night after night we lie in each other's arms, clung together, joyous, like the best wine, the sweetest honey, like a ripe fruit on a vine, split open.

But I am old now, Shaddai. My days are numbered on your earth. When I am gone, what will she do? Will her people take her back? Will they even know her, after all this time? No. You must help me, Shaddai. You must find a way to keep her here when I am gone, so that she is watched over and respected as one of our own people.

You have seen her. You know the way she laughs. The way she tosses her hair back. The way her hips move when she walks, like water. Who could have imagined that so old a woman as me would find such love, so late in life? Think of her in the morning, first waking up. Think of the way she turns to me. This is a woman who was not made to be alone. Find someone to care for her, so that when I am in Sheol I will not have to worry about her.

I think the best choice is Boaz, my late husband's kinsman. He visits the holy ones at their shrine, and has never married. Boaz owns much land but he has no children. He walks like a man who has never known a woman. He is kind and gentle and when I think about him with my Ruth, having children, I see it as a blessing for both of them. So please, Shaddai, hear my prayer and find a way for the two of them to be together, so that I won't have to worry about her when I'm gone. But, god of my people, please, please, remember this old woman, and do not do it too soon."

The Genizah of Dreams :~

~: The Wooden Box ☾ :~

Jonathan and David made a pact, because Jonathan loved David as himself. Jonathan took off the cloak and tunic that he was wearing and gave them to David, together with his sword, bow, and belt.   1 Samuel 18:3-4

"Soon it will be over," he said out loud. That was one of the nice parts about being old, he thought, that he could talk to himself and sing to himself, whenever he felt like it, and nobody paid any attention. Once scribes followed him, copying down every word he said, and they wrote down the words of every song he sang. But so much had happened. So much loss. "Once I danced, naked, in front of the Ark of the Covenant. And now I can hardly walk."

David looked over at the servant girl they had chosen to take care of him. She was fast asleep on cushions in a corner of the room. In a niche in the wall three oil lamps burned, and by the door a tall lampstand stood, with seven lamps burning. The sound of the priest's horn, announcing the night prayer, broke the stillness in the room. Unable to sleep, David sat on the edge of his bed and reached for the harp that hung on the wall, the harp that King Saul had given him, all those years ago. But his fingers hurt when he began to pluck its strings. Besides, he didn't want to wake the girl, so he hung it back on its peg on the wall.

Across the room, beside the lampstand, was a small wooden chest. He had ordered it made many years before, to look like a small Ark, an Ark without carrying poles, an ark to hold his most precious possessions. He shuffled across the room and slowly lowered himself to the hard stone floor. Kneeling in front of the chest, with trembling hands, he lifted the golden lid, with its two cherubim facing each other, their wings outspread. Inside was a faded purple cloak, neatly folded, and beneath it a tunic of red embroidered with silver and gold. He lifted them to his face and smelled them. He pressed them to his cheek. He wept then, and as he wept he softly sang the end of the song that he had sung to himself for all these years:

"My brother Jonathan, you were most dear to me. Your love was wonderful to me, more than the love of women."

II Samuel 1:26

The Genizah of Dreams ∻

~: The Holy One ⚎ :~

He tore down the cubicles of the male prostitutes in the House of YHWH, at the place where the women wove coverings for Asherah.   II Kings 23:7

I pour oil in my lamp, pull up the wick, and light it. My shadow looms up on the wall at the back of my chamber, on the hanging my mother wove for me on her loom, a trellis of vines, their grapes thick in clusters. I have bathed in the sacred pool. I sprinkle incense on an ember from the sacred fire. I have prayed as the priests taught me when first I came here. I have opened my body to God. I have become His messenger, my wings open wide to all who come in prayer.

In the doorway, I sit and wait. Men pass, gaze, pass. Then one stops for a moment. I smile. He looks away, then looks back at me again. I nod and say, "Come, friend. Come, grapple with me as our father Jacob grappled with an angel." He smiles. He pauses, then starts to turn away. I know why. He has heard the railing of the prophets in the marketplace. But what do they know, old men who tell us we must only serve God with the words of our mouths? And he has listened to the priests when they read their new laws. Why have they forgotten how to pray with their bodies? Why have they forgotten the true words of God, who made us whole and told us we are good?

In this House, I am God's messenger. I open my body in prayer for all who come to me. And he turns, he turns back to me. His smile, a shy one, tells me that he is new to Judah, to the city, a pilgrim, come from afar, from Gath, Beersheba, or from somewhere perhaps in Israel. The cloth of his robe is coarse, his sandals are worn. But the look in his eyes, his smile as it rises up, aren't they the opening to a prayer?

I stand. We are the same height. I reach out my hand and he takes it. Then I lead him into my chamber. "How good it is," the song singers tell us, "for brothers to lie together in love." Already my heart and my body are opening to him. "My name is Beriah," I whisper to him. "Shelesh," is all that he says back, his voice warm and deep but quivering. From the way that he says his name I can tell that he is from the north.

"How beautiful you are, man of Israel. With hair like the black of night, and eyes like stars, shining for me. You are tall as the cedars of Lebanon this House was built from. And you are beautiful as a mountain stag, standing strong before me."

He looks away, afraid. Then he reaches out a hand to me. I take it and place it on my heart. He strokes my cheek. Then his lips, red as pomegranates, sweet as honey, press against mine. And his tongue, that singer of psalms, seeks out my own sweet singing voice. And, clasped in each other's arms, we sink to my mat, pressed upon soft cushions. And we breathe together, as God first breathed into Eve and Adam to give them life. And I open my heart to him. My wings wrap round him. I kiss his ear and whisper to him.

"We are one and holy, each in himself, created in the image of God, female and male woven together in one flesh. We are Jerah and Naam, together when the world was new. And we are David, who danced before the Ark of God, we are David and Jonathan, the two of them loving God through each other's kisses."

He has buried his face in the side of my neck. He rolls on top of me. I stroke his back, tenderly. He pushes himself up on his elbows and looks down at me. I take his face in my hands and kiss his brow. We begin to move, together. And I sing this song to him, the song that the priests taught me when first I came to this House of God-loving.

"Come now with me, my beloved, into the place of light that births darkness, and the darkness that renews the light. We are the tablets of the law, side by side. We are the two pillars before this Holy House. We are consecrated unto God. We are Israel and Judah, united again. We are an offering to God. Our bodies are a holy prayer."

~: The Chariot of Flames ע :~

As they kept on walking and talking, a fiery chariot with fiery horses suddenly appeared and separated one from the other; and Elijah went up to heaven in a whirlwind. Elisha saw it and he cried out, "Oh, father, father, Israel's chariots and horsemen." II Kings 2:11-12

I sent My chariot for him, for Elijah. I swept him up in My embrace. He was not the first and he will not be the last.

I sent My chariot for Elijah the prophet. I swept him up in My embrace. He was not the first and he will not be the last. And all that was mortal of him was transmuted. And all that was timeless in him was transformed. I made of him something new, a being neither human nor angel, but both of them.

I swept him up in My embrace. I made of him a being both angel and human, because of the love that he and his beloved Elisha shared. And I sent him forth to carry this love to all of his people. I sent him out into the world. In every time, in every place, he is there to comfort his people, Elijah the Tishbite, a prophet from Gilead.

And when Elisha died I sent My chariot for him too, beloved of Elijah. Yes, I sent horses and chariot of flames. I sent it for Elisha the son of Shaphat and I kept him with Me. I kept him with Me until his time had come. And now is his time. And now is his season. Now I send him forth into the world, to carry the message of love to the people of Israel. I send him into the world to sing to Me a new song, to write for Me a new psalm of praise, a blessing of peace and love for all people, and for all the world.

The Genizah of Dreams ~

~: The Secret of the Text פ :~

As they took out the silver that had been brought to the House of YHWH, the priest Hilkiah found a scroll of YHWH's teachings given by Moses.

II Chronicles 34:14

Hilkiah and those whom the king had ordered went to the prophetess Huldah.   II Chronicles 34:22

Hezekiah the son of Ahaz, king of Judah, purified the House of God and ordered the Passover celebrated as it had not been celebrated since the time of Solomon. Then he summoned all the scribes to Jerusalem. "Bring all of our sacred books, those from Judah and from the remnant of Israel, destroyed by Assyria, bring them all to this House, and make of them a holy text for all the people."

The king appointed two scribes to do this work, Joram from the tribe of Judah, and Elad from the remnant of the kingdom of Israel. They took the scrolls from Israel and Judah, the annals of the two lands, the *Book of Jashar*, and the *Book of the Wars of YHWH*, and all the stories of our ancestors. Joram and Elad took the scrolls and lay them side by side. Passage by passage they read them, and wove portions together, making out of them one scroll, in the archive of the temple, next to the house of the King.

As they worked together, side by side, Joram and Elad found favor in each other's heart. In the beginning their work was thick of seam and irregular. But as they worked and grew to love each other, year after year, with ink on parchment, reading and transcribing, their words became fluid, and their minds wove words together as tightly as a carpet. And their hearts bound fast together through their work. When it was done the king had the chief priest read the scroll of their work, on the great festival of Sukkot. All week he read, in the main court of the temple. All Judah, and the remnant of Israel, heard the words of God as if for the first time, the words that Joram and Elad had made whole by their love for each other in the service of God.

Many years later, in the reign of Hezekiah's great-grandson Josiah, the priest Hilkiah found a scroll of God's teachings in the temple. He gave it to Shaphan the scribe, who brought it to the king. And Josiah went to the prophetess Huldah, who told him what to do with the scroll. The king read the scroll to all the people, in the court of the House of God. And the people dedicated themselves to God. And none of them knew that it was the tenderness of Joram and Elad they were hearing, who were seated together side by side for seven years, reading and writing, weaving together ancient words, till one long scroll was filled, and twenty-one copies made of it.

The Genizah of Dreams :~

◌: In the Vineyard of Dreams ✡ :◌

Let me sing for my beloved a song of my lover about his vineyard.   Isaiah 5:1

And let not the eunuch say, "I am a withered tree." For thus said YHWH: "As for the eunuchs who keep My sabbaths, who have chosen what I desire and hold fast to My covenant – I will give them, in My House and within My walls, a monument and a name better than sons or daughters. I will give them an everlasting name which shall not perish."   Isaiah 56:3-5

Hoshea, king of Israel, owned great estates, from Dan to Bethel, with vineyards and orchards and fields of rich grain. The scribe for his vineyards was Neriyahu the son of Mattan, made a eunuch as a youth, to serve the royal family. When Israel fell to the Assyrians, when its people were taken off in exile, an exile from which they did not return, some escaped their conquerors' wrath, hiding in the hills and fleeing south to Judah. Neriyahu the son of Mattan was among them

Knowing that the people of Judah did not make eunuchs, ridiculed them, and did not allow them in their temple, Neriyahu wished he could take off his eunuch's earrings and bracelets and dress himself as any other man. But he had been made a eunuch as a youth, so he remained beardless and with a voice neither male nor female, but sweet as the voice of an angel. Thousands of Israelites swarmed into Judah and Jerusalem, and work was hard to find, especially for a eunuch. Finally, through a distant kinsman, Neriyahu found work as tutor for the daughters of the king of Judah's minor concubines.

One day, crossing the courtyard of the king's house, Neriyahu came upon a crowd standing in rapt attention, listening to the words of Isaiah the son of Amoz, a prophet of God. For a moment the eyes of the prophet and the eunuch met. From that day forward, whenever he heard that the prophet was preaching, Neriyahu would go to listen to him. Each time they encountered each other, for a moment, when their eyes met, the two men would pause, nod, and share a single breath. Years passed, without them ever exchanging a word. The prophet's wife died, the eunuch's charges grew and younger daughters of other concubines took their place, learning from him the basics of reading and writing. And one day, as he was leaving the courtyard, the prophet tripped and fell, as he was walking past Neriyahu, who caught him, cradled him, and gently lowered him to the ground. And just as breath passed from eye to eye, so too now did it pass from body to body, the enlivening breath of God that fills us all.

Neriyahu escorted Isaiah home, limping, and sent out the prophet's servant to call for a healer. She came and tended to the prophet, but after she had gone, Neriyahu remained, to care for Isaiah as his twisted ankle healed. He sent word to the king's house that he would not be returning, and remained in that house for days, telling stories to the older man, who was greatly in pain. Isaiah's favorite stories were about the vineyard that Neriyahu had managed, stories he told so vividly that Isaiah felt that they were there together, in the warmth of day, walking the rows, tending the vines together, he on an ankle already healed. And from the touch of caring hands, and from Neriyahu's stories, love sprung up between the two men, a eunuch and a widowed prophet. Neriyahu became Isaiah's scribe and companion, attending to him in all ways. And from time to time, when the spirit of God filled him, words came to Isaiah that were for all the people of Israel, and yet just for Neriyahu, the prophet's beloved.

The Genizah of Dreams :~

~: From a Shelf on the 613th Floor ק :~

It is Wisdom calling, Understanding raising her voice.
She takes her stand at the topmost heights.

Proverbs 8:1-2

Huldah spent all of her time tutoring students up in fourth heaven. Her area of expertise was training advanced teachers who were getting ready to incarnate again. After more than thirty centuries in heaven she rarely thought about her own last life on Earth, but every hundred years or so something would come over her, nostalgia, sorrow, regret, delight. Then she'd find herself heading up to the archives in the center of sixth heaven, climbing the great spiral staircase, its stairs of crystal glowing from within. Oh, the size of it! Thousands of levels, each one as large as an ocean. And the rows, the racks, the shelves, the stacks, room after room after room of them.

Huldah mounted the stairs till she came to her floor. She pushed through the high silver doors and headed toward her section. A gilt sign hung from the luminous amber ceiling, which read, "Prophecy, Song, Poetry: Hebrew." She turned left and then right, stopping at a smaller sign that read, "Prophets, singers, poets: female."

There were hundreds of volumes there. None of them had been preserved down on Earth. Many of them had been written by students in the school that Sheerah and Shulamit had founded, and others came from the many forgotten women who were prophets in Israel. She reached out a trembling hand for the nearest volume, which turned out to be *The Love Songs of Zeruiah, the Daughter of King David.*

Zeruiah was David's youngest child, his daughter with Bathsheba, named for his own sister. Like her father, Zeruiah was a poet, a singer of songs. All of her songs were written to women. Huldah had forgotten how beautiful they were, so beautiful that she couldn't put down the scroll. Instead, she took it to a study carrel at the end of the aisle and spent the rest of the afternoon poring through it, from beginning to end. She was so moved that she forgot all about her own lost books. No, it was only at twilight, when Zeruiah's book was back on its shelf, when Huldah was heading down the aisle, when the firmament above her was flooded with angels chanting the evening prayers, that she remembered, with a flash of anger that there was no Book of Huldah in the scriptures, as there were books named for Jeremiah and the other prophets who were men.

Like lightning, her anger flared, then passed. Wistfully, Huldah continued down the great stairs, heading back to her residence. "Funny," she thought, "that I can still be knocked off center by how history has unfolded." Then she stopped in her tracks and started to laugh, out loud. A passing angel paused for a moment, puzzled. Looking up at it, Huldah laughed again, remembering that every word ever spoken, every book ever written down on Earth, sits on a shelf of aquamarine, in the archives of heaven. "Nothing is ever lost," she said to herself, smiling. "Everything is waiting to be found again, in its own right time."

The Genizah of Dreams ∽

~: In the Heart of the Heart of the Palace ד :~

Thereupon Esther summoned Hathach, one of the eunuchs whom the king had appointed to serve her.

Esther 4:5

You think I would be grateful to my uncle, who sent me off to fulfill my destiny. But looking back on it now, it seems to me that Uncle Mordechai used my beauty to help free our people, never realizing how that freedom would enslave me.

Perhaps you think I should be grateful to the king, who raised me up from obscurity to queenship, a lovely Hebrew orphan girl, now imprisoned in his palace for life. Yes, I came in my own way to love Ahasuerus, but the One who allowed me to save our people granted me neither children nor continuing purpose.

No, looking back on my life in the walled gardens of the king's palace, the one I am grateful to is Hathach, the eunuch the king appointed to serve me.

And isn't it always this way, that women like me and men like him find each other? Isn't it always this way, that beneath our obvious differences, a queen and a slave, that we found each other and became the closest of friends, in the heart of the heartless king's palace?

Nights when everyone was asleep, we would sit up talking like two sisters, sipping spiced wine and telling stories. Trapped in the palace, I sat in rapt attention as Hathach told me stories about his adventures outside the palace walls, the shops and stalls he went to, to fulfill one or another of my requests, for perfume, henna, kohl, or new fabrics. And then the stories I liked best, about the men he met in the market, their homes, their gardens, their beds, those hungry lovers of a single afternoon. And I would regale him with stories about the palace, about the king, about the things I learned from sitting quietly and listening. And sometimes, when we had nothing better to do, we would open up trunks and boxes and pull out all my clothing and makeup. And the two of us, laughing till kohl-streaked tears poured down our cheeks, would dress up in ridiculous costumes and parade about my room, inventing stories to go with our disguises. And if people think about me, years from now, the savior-prisoner of our history, I hope that they too will dress up in outlandish costumes with their best beloved friends, drink spiced wine, eat silly candies, and laugh through the night till dawn arrives on tipsy feet of the softest strongest pink.

The Genizah of Dreams :~

~: The World to Come 𝕍 :~

Lo, I will send the prophet Elijah to you.   Malachi 3:23

Elijah's boyfriend Danny is much cuter in person than he looks on the news. I met him last week at an art opening. He's shorter than I thought he'd be, but he has a great smile, and his eyes are so amazing. They're the greenest green that I've ever seen. Don't you think that he and Elijah make a really nice looking couple? Danny is so fair and Elijah is so dark. Remember how upset the Ashkenazi rabbis were, when they found out the prophet is Sephardic? But he showed them, didn't he, the minute he started talking Yiddish? I wonder where he learned it.

Oh, but it was Danny I wanted to tell you about. He was really nice at the opening, totally natural and friendly. We walked around for a while and talked about the paintings. I didn't get to talk to Elijah at all though. He was in the other room all evening, having an intense conversation with the artist. The next day

I was talking with this guy at my gym about meeting Danny. He told me that his college roommate dated him for a few months during their sophomore year, and that Danny isn't very well endowed, but he's a fabulous kisser.

The Genizah of Dreams ∻

~: The Messiah's Study ת :~

See, a time is coming, declares YHWH, when I will raise up a true branch of David's line. He shall reign as king and shall prosper, and he shall do what is just and right in the land.   Jeremiah 23:5

That evening a fiery seraph brought the messiah a message from seventh heaven, a message from God Herself: "Your time is at hand." This was what she'd been waiting for since she'd been created, eons before. Trembling, the messiah sent off the seraph with a message for her council of advisors. "Come. Now."

Miriam arrived just as the last golden light faded into the turquoise radiance that is night in sixth heaven. Sheerah, Dinah, and Huldah soon followed. She'd set the table with a bottle of the finest blue wine from second heaven. The women settled in, none of them saying a thing. Dinah broke the silence. "They'll be surprised down there, won't they, when they discover who their anointed really is?" she said, with a grin. They all laughed and clinked their glasses. "But what a glorious day it will be," Miriam added. Then, as was their custom, Huldah unrolled a book she'd written in heaven, *The Coming of the Woman of Light*, and they began their study session, for the very last time.

"And the daughter of David will reign in peace in Jerusalem, forever and ever," Huldah read. "In the name of the Radiant Mother of All. Blessed be Her name."

The Genizah of Dreams ~

Al-Andalus

∼: TALES OF AN IMAGINARY SPAIN :∼

Al-Andalus :~

~: **Remembering Spain** :~

A poem to be shared in bed, on the Sabbath

There was a time when we could do this, you see
Kiss other Jewish boys and men with impunity
Stroke their cheeks and pull them close
Against the law
Untying their sashes
So that we could slip warm hands onto their nakedness
And raw, passionate, hungry, rejoicing
we could sink with them on cushions to the floor
Bathed in streaming light through latticework
Reflecting Spanish heat
We would writhe, moan and cry out in our shared release
To God

～: ～

Blessed are You
Who makes such passion
Spanish poets and rabbis once called out
But conquest, conversion, death, or
　banishment
Lost us our Iberian Hebrew and Arabic-
　speaking brethren
And their sacred hymns of praise

Yes, once we could do this, once long ago
You see
kiss other Jewish boys and men
With lust, love, need, and with fidelity
To the deeper laws
Not of Sinai but of the heart
Revealed to us by divine reason
As just, right, true
And certainly the highest gift of our creator

So now again, in this day
Poets, lovers, psalmists, painters,
Scholars and bakers, potters and dancers
Bend close your bearded Jewish faces to
　other men
Breathe in the breath God-given
In praise of all creation
And to the handiwork of that long sixth day

Al-Andalus ～

To the man whose tongue now shapes wet
   words in your mouth
Wet wordless words of holy praise

Hear O Israel, who wrestled with an angel
Never was there a day in which I loved you
   more than now
Naked in my arms and calling out
Hallelujah

Al-Andalus :~

~: Reading "Shemot" :~

"The most important thing in this portion is seldom noticed," Rabbi Solomon ibn Uzair said, as he lay on a pile of cushions beside his lover Joseph. A small scroll of the Torah lay open in front of them, rolled to the beginning of the book of *Shemot*. Beyond the rabbi's study, in the square below, they could hear the sounds of the market, heavy wooden wheels of carts, and the horses that pulled them, sounding on the hard dry earth of summer. The cacophony of shoppers' voices, the cry of vendors calling out their wares, all mixed together and rose up into the room, bringing the heat of day into that chamber, lit only by the shafts of light that poured through the open lattice-work shutters.

"And what is that?" Joseph the younger man asked his lover, running a slim dark hand over the rabbi's forearm, running against the grain of coarse hair, his own hand then stopping over the page, like a golden *yad* above the text, pointing. The rabbi smiled and let his own hand caress his partner's shoulder. "Joseph, you aren't paying attention to what I told you last week, when we were finishing *Bereshit*."

"How can I pay attention, when the day is so hot and dusty?" Solomon leaned over the young man to grab a pitcher off the small round copper table that sat beside the divan. Tall and thin, the pitcher of green glass was filled with water, which he poured into the two empty cups on the table.

"You mean the water?" Joseph asked. "There's water in *Bereshit* and now there's water here, the river." The rabbi smiled. "You've got the right idea. But go back to the text and read for me." Stumbling over the Hebrew words, Joseph read the first passage. The room was still. He could feel his lover's impatience with him, in the controlled rasp of his breathing. These were moments when he hated Solomon, only five years older, but acting as if he were the wisest man in all of Jewry. He glared at him for a moment. The older man's hand extended over the open scroll, about to point out what he had missed.

"Don't! Let me find it," Joseph snapped. Solomon pulled back his hand. He hated it when his temper rose, especially when it rose up against Joseph, so sweet, so good to him. Without waiting, Joseph dived back into the text. He read slowly, with an edge of hostility in his voice. And then he came to the beginning of the story about Moses, to the fifteenth word,

Al-Andalus ∾

and the sixteenth. "Ki Tov!" "That's it, isn't it? That's what you wanted me to see. That *Bereshit* begins with God saying Ki Tov about creation, and now, at the very beginning of *Shemot*, Moses's mother says that about her baby son!"

Solomon reached out a broad hand and rumpled Joseph's hair. Usually when he did that Joseph hated it. "I'm not your horse," he'd snap, "so get your fingers out of my mane." But this time, the heat, the words of Torah, and the tender warmth of his lover's dark hand, telling him that he'd learned the lesson of the day, made him smile, grab that hand, pull it to his mouth and sink his teeth into the web between Solomon's thumb and index finger. "Ouch!" the rabbi shouted, pulling his hand away. But Joseph grabbed it back and licked where his teeth marks remained. "Ki Tov," he whispered, then licked it again, as Solomon, with his other hand, rolled up the scroll of the law and placed it on the table.

Al-Andalus :~

~: In Granada :~

Across the street, over the rooftop, in the next building, a young man in blue cooks his single dinner over a tiny flame. Perhaps a student, I saw him once in the marketplace, bent over a wooden tray of lemons from North Africa. Sidling up to him, smitten by his pale green eyes, by the ringlets in his beard, by his dark fingers, curled around a lemon, cradling it in his palm, I began to tremble. Such beauty should not be allowed. Without him noticing me, I followed him to a grain vendor's stall, and watched him purchase a handful of rice and a handful of beans. Then I lost him in the crowd, and now – curse and blessing – he lives across from me, in a tiny attic room, with a fireplace just big enough for a single iron pot to hang above the flames.

O the flames that rise up in me, that burn me, as he turns and bends, cutting something I cannot see, on a board that I can't see either. Only the rise and fall of his arm, the way that his shoulder muscles swell and then stretch out, the rest of him out of view through his tiny window.

Did he see me!? I turn to look down at my book, then look back, like David on his roof, captivated by Bathsheba. I would kill for him, like David did. But how much better it would be if he were the son of a king and came to me freely, like Jonathan came to David, swearing his devotion.

He is gone now. And so is my ability to read. The text before me, "Berachot," is meaningless. What blessings can come to me with him living across the courtyard? I will have my windows sealed. I will move my study to another room. Down to the small one that faces the street. It's cooler there anyway, in summer.

He is back. He has changed his robe. Now in brown, with lighter stripes, are they tan or gray, I cannot tell from here. This robe is looser, a little bit open in front. God of Israel, have mercy on me. Through the opening, as he turns for a moment toward me, toward me without seeing me, a wash of dark hair, like a wave coming in on that beach near Cadiz, with all of its sailors, beach that we visited when I was a boy, the beach where first I knew the direction my heart turned, toward the west, away from Jerusalem. I will sell this house. I will live all year outside the city walls with my mother, in her summer house, overlooking the olive groves.

Al-Andalus ∽

No, Ezra. Now you are being foolish. Open your book again. Read. Read and look out. Read and look out and recite the blessing your father taught you when you were a little boy, the blessing to recite when you see a king and his court. For if all the men of Israel are princes, this young man is surely a king, and the fire, his pot, and whatever he is chopping, are surely his retinue.

"Blessed are You, O Lord our God, King of the universe, who has given of Your glory to mortals." And tomorrow, I shall go shopping again, back to the same marketplace, where if I'm lucky, I'll see him again. But should I wear the red robe with the yellow sash, or the green one with gold? And which sandals? No, this is holy ground. I should go barefoot.

Al-Andalus :~

~: The Rabbi and the Court Physician :~

"Remember how we worried, twenty years ago, about what they would say in the city, Jews and even Muslims?"

"A rabbi and the court physician, setting up house together."

They both laugh, over their cups of wine, thinking back on how it was, and how it is, and how it will be, now that both of them are old. Neither one says, "Who will die first?" Each one hopes it will be the other, to spare him the pain of being left behind. And each one prays the prayer of long-time lovers, that they will fall asleep in each other's arms and die together, on a warm night when the sky is strewn with stars to help them find their way back home.

"Are you sorry? Do you ever have regrets?" the rabbi asks the doctor.

The doctor answers, more with his body, with the lift of his shoulders and the way they drop, and his eyes light up as he reaches across the small table to take his companion's hand. "Never."

"Not even about children?"

The doctor laughs. "Remember that time, when your mother was dying, and we sat with her and with your sisters, all of us gathered around her bed, your sisters and their husbands. We all were crying. I could tell from her breathing and her pulse that the end was near. And you took her hand and brought it to your lips and kissed it, and said to her, "Mother, I'm sorry that I didn't give you grandsons." Remember how she pulled herself up on her pillow and said, "Dear, your pupils are your sons. And you've had so many."

The rabbi laughs as he pours the two another cup of wine from its glass decanter, an Egyptian glass decanter, decorated with garnets and pearls. "Remember the morning when you came to me in tears, because you'd found that first gray hair on your chest?"

"And you bent down and kissed me, right between my nipples, and you said, 'I'm sorry my love, but don't expect much sympathy from me.' And you pulled off your turban so that I could see your shiny bald head."

"See, it hasn't been so bad."

"Bad? All that I can see is good. I can't imagine what my life would have been like if we hadn't met."

Al-Andalus ∾

"You were already married to your patients. You would have just gotten more married."

"Don't flatter yourself," says doctor to rabbi, teasing. "I would have met someone else."

"I wouldn't have. I was happy with my studies, my writing and my teaching."

"Yes you would have. A man as beautiful as you can't stay single forever."

The rabbi blushes and pulls his hand away from his lover. "When I was half awake this morning I sensed you asleep beside me, and I felt as I did when we were first together. Then I woke up, looked up at the ceiling, and I remembered that we're old."

"The soul has no age, my love. And it's our souls that love each other. We're like David and Jonathan."

"Jonathan died young."

"We're like Abraham and Sarah."

"Which one of us is which?"

"We're like Moses and Aaron."

"They were brothers."

"Ruth and Naomi?"

"Ruth married someone else."

"Why are you making this so hard for me, rabbi? Is this how you treat your students?"

"Remember, doctor, that I was an innocent when we met."

"Innocent! Just because you were a virgin doesn't mean that you were innocent. You were the one who ravished me, remember?"

"Well, maybe I did, but not until you'd kissed me and slid your arm around my back and then kissed me again."

"How could I resist? Those lips were made for kissing."

"Were?"

"Wait. Who kissed who this morning? And who pushed who away and said, 'Not till I rinse out my mouth?'"

"And you call yourself a physician? It isn't sanitary."

"And what exactly did you get in your mouth last night that rendered your lips and tongue and mouth unsanitary?"

The two of them laugh.

"Thank you dear. Do you have anything else to say?" Said with a twinkle in his large dark eyes.

"Just thank you."

"For bringing home this wine?"

"No, silly. Thank you for everything."

Then the rabbi pours his companion another cup of wine, from the Egyptian decanter decorated with garnets and pearls, that was a gift from the king to his court physician. And they raise their cups to each other's lips, just as they did on the night when they first were living together under the same red tiled roof in Cordoba, more than twenty years before.

Al-Andalus :~

∽: Erev Shabbat :∽

Fridays I hate
The hectic rush to get ready for a day of rest
Absurd as those mornings when my mother
    frantically cleans the house
Because the Moorish cleaning woman is
    coming

And I hate it here too
In the bath house

Folding my clothing
Wrapped in a long sheet
I crossed the foyer from the changing room
And there was Jonah
Standing beside a column
Talking to someone
But staring at me
And although he quickly looked away
He knew that I saw him looking

Longing

Then, in the steam room
Right after my massage
Climbing up to a higher row
Wanting to burn away
Sorrow, shame, even pity
There I see Aaron
Turning away from me
Pretending he didn't see me

But we all know
As scientists tell us
That something comes out of the eyes
A light, a ray
Perhaps the remains of the primal light
Of creation
It comes out of our eyes
And when we look at something
At someone
It touches them
And they feel it

So I could feel Jonah looking at me
Good Jonah, and kind
Just as I could feel Aaron looking at me
So handsome, and cruel
And just as I see Jonah in the moment

Al-Andalus ∼

before he turns away
And he feels that I've seen him
And done my own turn
I feel Aaron and Aaron feels me

What was God thinking
When He made this world?
Does this madness link us together
Like fathers and sons in their generations
That Jonah loves me
And I love Aaron
And Aaron loves whoever is willing and
    pretty
Round and around

But it is Friday afternoon
Erev Shabbat comes soon
So I will dip in chilly water
Dry myself off
Dress in my Sabbath best
And try not to think of God's unjoyful
    games
Till Havdalah is over
Till the spices and incense are put away
The candle snuffed in wine
The last song sung
Our day of rest
Over

Done
My restlessness
Come back again

Al-Andalus :~

~: Before Arvit :~

My grandfather told me when I was a little boy, that if I watched while the priests were reciting their three-part blessing, that I would surely die. He whispered those words to me, in this very room, and then he pulled his prayer shawl over my head so that I could not see. I was almost a bar mitzvah boy before I was courageous enough to look, and to this day I am always a little bit nervous when I do it, which I always do. So it was, this morning, that I peered up through the folds in my own prayer shawl, and I saw him standing there, the visitor, that cousin of the rabbi everyone has been talking about, come all the way from Egypt to teach here.

His hands were raised in priestly benediction, fingers split and spread beneath his prayer shawl. On either side of him two other kohanim stood, hands raised but hidden, in the same gesture. To his right, my mother's cousin Judah, and to his left, the rabbi's son-in-law, Omar. Both of them were taller than he, and I wondered about his age. And then, all of a sudden, his tallit slipped down over his arms, just as they began the third blessing. And I saw his face, face of a man my own age, or slightly older, a dark intense face, large of nose, thick of beard, high of brow. I meant to look down, but in that brief moment – he looked out over the congregation, and his eyes caught mine. I should have looked down, but my eyes were locked in his gaze. I could not look away. Then they began the third blessing. "May God show you kindness and grant you peace." And he did something that nearly did kill me. He smiled. He smiled a slightly crooked smile, a devastatingly wide and beautiful smile. I could swear it wasn't the light of the lamps burning overhead that illuminated the room, but his smile, shot into my heart like the sun's arrows at dawn. Shot through an opening in the shutters of my window, awakening me in my bed. His arms raised above his head in ancient blessing, his tallit slipped down on his thick dark arms, this rabbi from Fostat smiled at me.

This is why I got here so early, so much before the evening service begins. This is why I am standing in my place, long before my brothers have gotten here, who always arrive before me, and tease me about it. And this is why I am standing with my back to the ark, facing the doorway, so that I can see him when he comes in. But what will I do if he doesn't come? If

Al-Andalus :~

he comes but doesn't see me? If he sees me but does not smile again?

My grandmother, alone, up in the women's balcony, waves down at me. I nod up to her, too nervous to wave back. And then he comes in, his arm linked through his cousin's. They are talking, but his eyes are darting around the room. My heart swells. And he sees me. He sees me and – he smiles again, that same smile, now perhaps even broader, if that is possible. And I feel the muscles of my face pull my own face up into a smile, faster than a runner making his way from city to city on foot, faster than the swiftest horse on a battlefield – as he slips his arm out from his cousin's – as he pauses and drops his arms to his side. And takes a long slow breath, then begins to walk toward me, beneath the large golden oil lamps, newly lit by the sexton.

Al-Andalus :~

~: The Vizier :~

From across the courtyard Naphtali could hear his mother calling out to him. He ignored her for as long as he thought he could, and then called back, as if he'd just noticed her cry, "Yes, Mother. What is it?"

He knew what it was. "Come here, this very instant!" He put down his book and shuffled through the courtyard. There, in the reception room, his mother stood beside a four-foot tall lemon tree in a wooden tub. Its lemons were shiny, each one oiled and polished. He sighed. "Look at this, Tali. Isn't it beautiful?" He frowned. "Two days ago it was those giant lilies. Two days before that it was crocuses. When will he stop?"

"Naphtali ibn Yakub! The vizier is giving you a great honor."

"Mother, come on. You know what the vizier wants."

"And I know what you should want too."

Naphtali paused and carefully thought about how to answer. "Mother, you were married off to Father with no say in the matter. And look where you are now."

Her eyes shot wide open. She was tongue-tied for a moment, and in that moment her youngest son went on.

"So why are you trying to sell me off to the vizier, who will cast me off when he's tired of me, with no laws to protect me and no sons to care for me?"

Zipporah, his mother, took a step back, shocked at what her favorite son had just said. True, her husband had long ago tired of her, but that wasn't all that marriage was about. And this wasn't just any man who was courting her son. This was the Jewish general and vizier to the Muslim king of Granada.

Now the mother paused to weigh out her words. Seeing on her face the pain he'd just caused her, Naphtali reached out a long slim hand to one of the lemons. "It is a very thoughtful and beautiful gift. But if I don't write him back this time, what will he send next? The palm tree that Deborah sat beneath? The oak tree where Abraham and Sarah set up their camp?"

Zipporah laughed. "And today's poem is even more beautiful than the last one." She'd been holding the small rolled up parchment behind her back, which she now handed it to him, with a flourish.

Al-Andalus :~

"Mother, how could you read what he sent me?"

"Naphtali, it's a mother's duty to watch out for her children."

"Watch out? You know what he wants. Me, naked, bent over."

Zipporah's hands shot up to her face. The boy was right. And yet here, the most powerful Jewish man in all of Spain was sending her beautiful son poems and gifts. Not that they were poor. Her husband took good care of them, although he was almost never at home. But...

Naphtali read through the short poem, once, and again, smiling at the vizier's words, so well put together, intricate as the carved scrollwork that ran around the study room in the great synagogue, that room where the visiting vizier had first seen him.

"But why is it always about my eyes, or my skin? Why does he always compare me to something else? To some silly fawn, or a gazelle. I'll tell you why, Mother! Because he doesn't know me. He's making me up, to satisfy his own desire. And if I write him back, if I go to him, I'll be just like all those other boys."

"But you could care for him."

"Mother! Does he care for me? If he did, he'd stop writing and stop sending me things. He doesn't know me and he doesn't care for me. And we live in modern times now. It's not like it was when you were growing up. I don't have to go to him, on my hands and knees, like a beggar."

"Just consider, Naphtali."

"I am. And I have. I'm not his servant. And you know him. You know what everyone says about him. In a week or two he'll see someone else, and he'll write to him and send him things. And I'll be completely forgotten."

Zipporah sighed. This son of hers, this wiry wily boy, her last born, could go in a single moment from being petulant and immature to being wiser than all of her older sons, Reuben, Simon, Gideon, and even Abraham, the eldest, who looked out for all of them. "Naphtali, just don't be hasty about this. Make sure you know what you're doing. Such a man as the vizier shouldn't be toyed with."

"What about me being toyed with? I can't believe you. Pimping me out to him? Your own child."

"Naphtali. How dare you talk to your mother like that. You go to your room and stay there till you're called for dinner."

Dropping his head in mock shame, taking one last look at the lemon tree in its tub, Naphtali turned and shuffled out to the courtyard and back to his sunny room. He'd seen the vizier many times, in synagogue, in the streets, on his high black horse, surrounded by his guards. He was a tall and very handsome man. And Naphtali knew what the vizier could do for him. All of his former boys were set up in good positions. He knew that.

In his room he went back to the text he was studying, "Pirke Avot." The Hebrew wasn't always easy to read. But he turned to a verse he remembered from the last time he read it. "Beware of rulers, for they befriend someone only for their own benefit; they act friendly when it benefits them, but they do not stand by someone in his time of need." Yes, that was the vizier. And then he turned back to another verse. "Accept a teacher upon yourself and remove yourself from uncertainty."

Naphtali closed his eyes. He was back in the study hall again, sitting bent over a book. And Samuel the rabbi was standing behind him, pressed close and leaning over his left shoulder, a dark finger pointing to a line of text. Fire was burning up between the rabbi's chest and his back, where they touched. Flames were beginning to flicker on his shoulder, where the rabbi's arm rested. And the smell of him, the smell of his beard, curled and scented. The soft whisper on the side of his cheek, of his breath. That was what he wanted. Not the vizier. Not power. But wisdom. Yes, that was what he was after now. He was certain of it. "And if not now, when?" he read, from Rabbi Hillel, there on the same page.

Al-Andalus :~

~: In the Marketplace :~

"Don't look now, but there's the boy I was telling you about," Moses said to his cousin Rebecca, grabbing her forearm, as the two sat side by side on the edge of the fountain in the central marketplace.

"If you didn't want me to look," Rebecca hissed back, yanking her arm away, "then why did you tell me?"

"I don't want you to be obvious, that's all," he whispered back. "Coming toward us in green, with the white turban."

"How is this?" Rebecca scratched the side of her nose, casually, and then turned to the right as if she were simply stretching her neck muscles. "Oh. I see what you mean," she whispered back. "But why do you always go for one of them? What's wrong with Jewish boys? This city is full of them."

The tall broad-shouldered young man they were staring at passed them by, oblivious. Moses groaned. "He comes by here every day. But he never sees me."

"You're not answering my question. The last one was a Muslim, and the one before that was a Christian, the tall one with sandy hair and the space between his front teeth. And then there was another Muslim. What was his name? Selim? The one whose body didn't fit into his clothes."

"Come on, Rebecca. You liked him too. All those muscles."

"I liked him, but I didn't want to marry him. Just pinch that big round ass of his."

"I wanted to do more than pinch."

"You always do. But look what happened with Mufid. And Mustafa. And Ishmael."

"That's not fair. I just haven't found the right one yet."

"And what will it take to make him right? That you spend half your time in bed with him and the other half writing terrible poems."

"You said you liked them."

"I did not. I said that they were very evocative."

Moses looked crushed. First the young man he was enamored of had gone by, and now these words from his cousin. "Well, you may not like them. But Ishmael did. And so did Selim. The last time I saw him he said that he kept them all and still reads them. He even showed them to his new boyfriend."

"I bet that made you feel just great. Dumped but turned into bedtime reading."

Al-Andalus :~

Moses laughed. "Well, I'd rather have been dumped by Selim than be betrothed to Gideon."

"It's not official yet. You know that. I told my mother that if they went ahead with it I'd join a convent!"

"There you have it. I just want to sleep with non-Jews. You're threatening to become one."

"It would be great. Can't you see my parents in synagogue, trying to live it down? Their only child, the granddaughter of one of Spain's most famous rabbis, has changed her name to Sister Perpetual Resentment, and moved into a convent."

Moses laughed. "Well, I'll do my best tonight with my mother. I'll tell her we sat here all day and you sobbed about not wanting to marry Gideon. It'll all get back to your father by lunch tomorrow. That's the day they always play backgammon, isn't it?"

Rebecca nodded, then tapped her cousin's arm. "How about that one? In blue. A nice Jewish boy."

"Nice. Maybe too nice. A good student and a good mama's boy, carrying her parcels. I like a boy with fire in him. A boy who's trouble. You can have him."

"Look again, Moses. Look at the way the back of his calves push against his robe as he walks. And look at the swell of his shoulders. I think you dismissed him too soon."

Her cousin turned around to watch the boy and his mother, she empty-handed, he carrying two heavy canvas bags. "Look at that butt of his. Maybe you're right. A Jewish boy could be nice for a change. Do you know him?"

Al-Andalus :~

~: The Hidden Mirror :~

The room they rent is in the back of the home of an old widow, the sister-in-law of the former rabbi. It's a large room, separate from the rest of the house, past the kitchen and down a dark hallway that leads out to the kitchen garden. And to that room they've brought their few possessions, to the back of the house, past ornate rooms that no one uses any longer. There they are creating, day by day, a refuge, a haven, their own first little home together, Saul a flute player for the vizier, and Amram, player of the stringed rebab, and a teacher in the synagogue.

In the yard, in the kitchen garden, they watch the last of widow's servants, a woman even older than she is, bent over the wild jungle of herbs, as they stretch a length of patterned cloth from Tangiers over the window.

"She comes out here to watch us, you know, and to listen to us when we make music," Saul says to Amram, as he knocks a rusty nail into one corner of the cloth with a large stone, which he passes to his lover.

"If we give her a little bit of a thrill, is that such a bad thing?" Amram says, with a laugh. Then the two step back to admire their handiwork, their choice of fabric, and the way the last afternoon light streams through it, painting dark and light through the cloth, now a flaming dance of arabesques. Light bouncing off the tiny wood-framed mirror on the opposite wall, above their bed.

They stand in the middle of their small room, their large world, hand in hand. Amram is humming and Saul recognizes the melody. It's part of the chant for the Torah portion of the week, "Ki Tisa." Amram must be teaching it to one of the rich men in the city, who will on Shabbat rise up in the synagogue and chant it himself, during the service. When Amram comes to a part that he knows, Saul joins him. It was a shared love of music that first brought them together, finding each other night after night in the same tavern, come to hear Husain ibn Sina, the most famous oud player in the city, a blind old man with fingers so long, caressing the strings, that they seem to have an extra knuckle.

"It's my favorite portion," Amram says to Saul. He can chant the Torah from beginning to end, and loves teaching the chants to others, to boys studying for their bar mitzvah, and to the rich men who pay for the privilege of chanting during the service.

"What do you like about it?" Saul asks, pulling away to straighten one side of the red and black Berber rug that covers the stone floor.

"We're in it. That's why I like it."

His lover looks puzzled. "People like us aren't anywhere in the Torah, Amram. We're forbidden."

Amram smiles. "Remember how you used to think, before we met, that you were alone in the world, the only one made like you, anywhere? Never imagining that Adam and Eve must have had sons and grandsons just like us. But now, in the street, in the market, in the bathhouse, the synagogue, you tug on my sleeve and whisper, 'He's one, isn't he?' and you're always right. Well, the Torah is just like that. You just have to know how to see. How to listen. Then you can find us."

Sitting down in a narrow alcove, on the edge of their bed, Amram closes his eyes, takes a long slow breath, and begins to chant in Hebrew, sound coming from the back of his long dark throat. "And Adonai would speak to Moses face-to-face, the way a man speaks to his fellow man."

His voice is rich and deep. It always moves Saul, who has settled down on their only seat other than the floor, a rickety old wooden stool that the widow gave them. "But where are we in that verse? I don't understand."

Amram smiles. "Perhaps God, the Divine Beloved, was courting Moses."

Rather than being comforted, Saul shudders. "Don't say that! It's not right."

Amram stifles a laugh. His tender lover, from so devout a family, still struggles with his nature, and he knows not to offend him, for offense can easily turn into rage, or, worse than rage, silence. He reaches out to Saul, who pulls back, as if the extended hand would burn him. "One more verse. Please," he begs. Saul gives him the smallest of nods.

"See, I've called by name Bezalel, son of Uri, son of Hur, of the tribe of Judah," Amram chants, slowly. "And I've filled him with the spirit of God in wisdom and in understanding and knowledge and in every kind of work, to form conceptions to make in gold and in silver and in bronze, and in cutting stone for setting and in cutting wood – for making things in every kind of work. And I, here. I've put Oholiab, son of Ahisamach, of the tribe of Dan, with him." That last part, about Oholiab, he chants a little louder, adding emphasis to the words, "I've put," and "with him."

Saul sits motionless. Amram is afraid that he's offended him again. But then a large smile erupts across his face, so wide that his teeth sparkle and his dark eyes shine. "Like us. Just like us, Amram. I hear what you're saying now. That God brought Oholiab and Bezalel together, just like he brought us together. To make everything for the tabernacle. To make the ark. To make something special. A sacred place. Just like our room." He's grinning and Amram stands and grabs him up in his arms. "Exactly. And now you hear it. Now you see it. The hidden mirror in the Torah, my love. That's always there. Waiting. Just like I was waiting for you last year, in Ayesha's tavern."

Now the last light of day has faded. Saul lights a single oil lamp, while Amram tunes the strings of his pear-shaped rebab. And in the flickering light, seated on their Berber rug, the songs of Saul's wooden flute and Amram's rebab, dance and marry, in their tiny room, their tabernacle, knees pressed together, face to shining face, like the cherubim on top of the holy ark, the place where God speaks from.

Al-Andalus :~

~: Before there was Law :~

Before there was law
There was love
Before there was Torah
There was a mother cradling her child in her arms
Before there were her arms
That tender child was carried in her body
And all was one

Before there was law
There was One
All of us cradled in God's arms
All of us loved
All of us carried in God's womb
All of us One

The lover leans close to kiss his beloved
And there aren't two there
Just one

The beloved returns that kiss
And the separation between the upper and
   the lower waters
Created by God on the second day
is reversed
Making One again

I saw Nehemiah in the street yesterday
Crossing through mud and splashed by
   horses
Spattered by mud
Nehemiah was not made filthy
And so it is with life
That nothing makes us filthy
If we are pure of heart

Before there was two there was One
Everything yearns itself back toward one
Like a child to its mother's arms
Like lover to beloved

Nehemiah kisses me
And in that kiss whole silent wet Torahs
Are revealed
And his hand on my cheek
Speaks every volume of the Talmud
And a night together in bed is the Zohar
the Book of Splendor

Al-Andalus :~

~: My Forsaken Garden :~

I cannot go into my own garden anymore. Each time that I do, he is there, the servant whose job it is to tend the lilies. He is dark and beautiful, and he looks up at me with golden eyes, golden like the sun at the height of day, leaping across the sky with the grace of a gazelle.

I cannot go into my own garden anymore. My wife asks me why. My children ask me why. What can I tell them? That he whose job it is to tend the lilies, whose name is like the finest oil, Ovadyah, that he looks up at me from his fragrant plants and smiles. He is a lily, a rose, a lily growing in a valley, a rose among thorns, calling out to me in that garden. And so I avoid him, I wander the hallways of my house, in order to avoid him.

I cannot go into my own garden anymore. I was happy once, and now I suffer. I was glad once and now my countenance is dark. At night, upon my couch, alone, I lie awake in agony, thinking of him, of Ovadyah. He is dark, and the curls of his hair are like hands reaching out to me. He has captured my heart. I am his.

I cannot go into my own garden anymore. I will post guards around it, to keep me out. I will build a wall around it with no windows, no gateways, and no doors. I will seal him into it and leave him there, for he is dark and beautiful. And I am pale and frightened.

I cannot go into my own garden anymore, without shaking. For I am Ovadyah's, and he knows it. Each time that I go into my garden, he, my servant, looks up at me with dark eyes, beckoning. And I falter, I stumble on the paving stones, I stumble over words like a boy first studying Torah. And he, a youth, swift as a gazelle, he comes toward me, smiling. "Master," he says, "Master, come and see the lilies, how full they are, how strong, and tall, so swollen with life, dripping pollen." And my hands tremble, and I clench my teeth, so as not to say, "O give me, Ovadyah, the kisses of your mouth. For your love is more delightful to me than any of these flowers."

No, I cannot go into my garden anymore. Or so I tell myself, just before dawn each day, just before I go down to it, step by stone carved step.

Al-Andalus ː~

~: The Christian :~

To Yunus, my esteemed friend and colleague,

You ask me in your recent letter for the news from your hometown, as if you were gone from here and would never return. But we have kept a place for you at our table, set with the glass bowl from Crete you so admire. And we count on you returning, we few poets of passion and poverty. We've met again, all twelve of us. Is that number an accident? Tribes, or disciples, fifty years ago this would not have happened, that Moors, Christians, and Jews, are gathered to share their poems. But times are changing, as we all keep saying, hoping that what changes will stay changed, although some of us are old enough to remember changes we do not want to see again, as I know you'll understand.

A poet read last night, a featured poet, come up from Granada, to share his newest work. And then, to honor him, several younger men, all inspired by his work, were invited to read their tributes to him. Last month I read here. Next month it might be you. But the identity of last night's guest I leave to your imagination. Tall, dark, a Muslim, one of those men who are known by reputation, but whose work leaves much to the imagination. You know him, though. I remember the things you said about him, that night in the tavern, the last time you were here.

He sought us out. Suddenly, in the right circles, we are worthy of attention, fashionable, a fad, I suppose. Those rowdy poor poets who use language in such outrageous ways, defying convention. So he read, and he read, and he read. And there was almost no time for his disciples to read. In a way, we weren't sad. Boring as he is, at least he has talent, or he had. But none of this is really what I want to write you about.

That boy was there again. Ambrosius, his name is. The tall one, slim, the one I wrote you about the last time. What am I to do, Yunus? He's captured my heart. He's half my age. His father, a merchant of fabric, has his own fleet of ships that ply the seas from here to Africa, Italy, Greece and even Egypt. Last time you said to let him know what I feel, but what good could come of that? I am as old as his father, as poor as the servant who carries his books and his cloak. He says that he admires my verses, but even worse, he is one of the minions of our honored guest. And, as you can tell from his name, he's a Christian.

What good can come of this? Nothing. Is it love? Or is it only folly, the capacity to send out my heart toward a ready object, a wall to paint its dreams on? Did I tell you about his hands, and his eyes, and the way that he walks? I'm sure I did, in every letter. That he's a Christian does not bother me. I would convert if I thought he would kiss me. That he's half my age doesn't bother me. I would send him off after a year, two years, just as long as I had the chance to taste him. And that he writes bad verse, common, pedestrian, does not bother me either. He could be illiterate, a fool. If only he would look at me. And so I hunger, and go unfed, while you and Daweed go on and on, writing and loving and sharing that big soft bed of yours. What should I do, my friend? Forget him? Stop going to those silly gatherings, that always make me doubt myself and my work when I get home? You tell me what to do and I will listen.

Your old and devoted friend, Zechariah ibn Daud, a silly Jewish poet

Al-Andalus :~

~: The Commandments :~

Joseph says, "'You shall not lie with a man as with a woman.' It's simple. When I'm with another man, I do it standing. Or kneeling." We all laugh.

Abraham says, "You and your men. Not me. It's the young ones I'm after, so as far as I'm concerned the commandment doesn't apply to me. I've never been with another man. Just boys."

We all laugh. "What about Abner?" I ask him.

"Well, maybe that once I sinned."

We all laugh again and Abraham asks me, "How about you, Manasseh? You're very quiet today. How do you approach the law?"

I look away, out the window to the garden in the courtyard of Joseph's new house. A fountain gurgles, water streaming over the edge. Flowers in pots are in blossom, all yellows and reds. A cat wanders through the rows of pots, an orange cat with white markings. I turn back to the room. Close my eyes. Some men don't struggle with this. They are philosophers and find their way toward love with reason. But I am the son of a rabbi, the grandson of a rabbi. My mother's father was a rabbi and I am a rabbi myself. I turn back to my companions, the three of us seated on cushions around a small brass table, table covered with wine and sweets, all of them dripping with drizzled honey. I reach for a layered square, dough layered with ground dates and nuts. It sticks to my fingers as I raise it to my lips. Almost too sweet, it crumbles in my mouth.

"When I was younger," I say to them, "This is what I told myself. That there are scores of commandments about the tabernacle, about offerings and sacrifices, and since the destruction of the temple we follow none of them. And there are only two commandments about being with another man. So, I used to tell myself, if I'm sinning in all those other ways, what are two more sins?"

They do not laugh. I thought that I was being funny.

"That was when you were young. What do you tell yourself now, Manasseh?"

"Sometimes I argue with myself, like a Babylonian rabbi. I say, the Torah tells us that a man with a gluttonous drunkard of a son may take him to the elders to have him killed. But those rabbis argued about the son until they decided that there was no way in which that law could ever be followed. So I go to the prohibition against men being with other men and I argue with it, just like those rabbis did, till I've found a way to bend it to my will. I have a wife, and I know what it's like, I tell myself, to be with a man. And for me, being with a man is never like being with a woman."

Joseph jabs his index finger up in the air. They both laugh. "That's not what I mean," I say. "What I mean is how it feels on the inside." They burst out laughing again. "That's not what I mean," I say again, peeved. "I mean – how I feel when I'm with a man, somewhere deep in my heart, is nothing like how I feel when I'm with my wife."

"Amen," Abraham says, lifting his glass of wine up over the table. "But you still haven't answered the question, Rabbi. How do you deal with the commandment today?"

I am silent. I think about Elisha, whom I'll meet this evening, so passionate and so wise. So tender, so loving. I remember once asking him this very question, not long after we first met, because, being ten years younger than I am, raised in a different era, he did not seem to have any struggle about this. I thought that he would tease me and call me old-fashioned, tell me he's never thought about it at all, but instead this is how he answered me. "The rabbis tell us that all the Jews who ever were and ever will be were standing together at Sinai when the Torah was revealed to us. So I say, if all of us were at Sinai, then Sinai is always happening, and in this very moment, God is revealing Himself to us." Then he leaned closer and kissed me, pulled away and said, "I know in my heart of hearts that that is not a sin. Don't you?"

"Rabbi, where are you?" Joseph said, bringing me back to the table from my reverie. I shrug. Such things cannot be put into words. A night with Elisha explains itself. And they know that. "Did you hear about the new tavern that's opened, by the Western Gate?"

"Tobias told me about it. Have you gone yet?"

Al-Andalus ∻

~: Twice a Heretic :~

"Kadosh, Kadosh, Kadosh," we say to You in prayer, three times over. "Holy, Holy, Holy." And now I find myself before You, at thrice the age of a boy who has had his bar mitzvah. I cannot count the times over all these years that I have awakened and called out to You, still in my bed, that I stand before You, God. I have thanked You for the purity of my soul, for the wonders of my body. I have praised and exalted You, over and over again, in words of my own, in synagogue, joined with my people in common prayer, Sabbath after Sabbath, festival after festival, fast day after fast day. I've read psalms and even written them to You, as all of my friends have, calling out to You, O God of Israel.

When I was twice the age of a bar mitzvah boy I remember asking the rabbi of my youth this question: "After all of these years of calling out to God, why hasn't He called back?" The rabbi's answer was simple. "To the prophet Elijah He spoke, we are told, in a still small voice." I knew nothing of still small voices. Our household was always filled with people, and our prayer halls are always jammed and noisy from men's prayers. Curious about how I would ever hear that still small voice, I asked my Christian friend Rolando about silence, for I had heard that Christian monks spend long periods of time alone, silent, in prayer. He told me what he knew, gave me a book of his to read, which invoked the same passages about the still small voice. So I found places to still myself, in the attic, the cellar, in the synagogue at times when no one else was there. Once, feeling very brave, I asked Rolando if I could go to church with him, and he took me, at a time when mass was not being offered. He led me to a tiny chapel, where candles flickered before an image of a saint. I was nervous and yet curious. He knelt and I stood in silence. But I did not hear Your voice, God, although we remained there a long time, and I have tried, in the middle of the night, when I wake, to feel my way to You in the silence, to open myself up to You, in the silence. But You never spoke back to me, God, not one single time in all of those years.

Once when we were boys, and he had just come back from mass, I remember Rolando telling me about the mystery of Jesus, how he was God Himself, come to earth, come into a human body. That he was born, suffered, and died for our sins. It did not make sense to me, why the Creator of all that is would have to do that. But it makes sense to me now.

The first time I saw him, God, come into a room, I felt as if a comet had shot its way down from the heavens, down across the sky, sending its fiery tail out behind it, illuminating the night. I felt as if that comet had flared its way across the sky and then careening downward, had slammed into my chest with the force of a gigantic cannon ball, crumbling my defenses, smashing through all of my protective walls, setting me on fire. Each time that I saw him, God, walking in the city, in the market, in the bathhouse, I burned. And if I saw him with any other men, such rage flamed up in me that I feared for my actions. And I ran from him, turned my back and fled each time I saw him. I am not a boy, God, as you know, and this foolish youthful passion is unseemly.

So why did You do this to me? Why didn't You just speak, as You spoke to the prophets, directly, or spoke to the rabbis of old, in a lesser voice, which we call the daughter of a voice? God, I would fall to my knees before You if you spoke to me in the great great granddaughter of a voice, in a voice so tiny that it would make a whisper sound like waves crashing on the shore, or the crack of lightning shattering the sky, or the thunder of horses across a plain, pulling iron chariots. Instead, you have come to me this way, turning me into a Christian. For now I understand what Rolando was telling me all of those years ago. You *do* enter the world. You *can* be born. But this time it is me who suffers, me who is dying, me who yearns to sin and live for my sins. What madness, to be twice a heretic, for now I believe like a Christian and not a Jew. But I cannot join their church for I do not believe that Jesus was Your only begotten Son, but Abdul.

Abdul ibn Rachman, the son of a minister to the king. Abdul ibn Rachman, even his name sends shivers through me. I ran from him. You know that I did. I turned and ran, double heretic that I am, falling in love with a Muslim. And now yesterday, in a voice so loud that I could not deny it, You called out to me through him, and I ran to You. A cart out of control, thundering down the Street of the Tailors, just as I was passing. I heard it before I saw it, and I threw myself up against a wall as it passed. But there ahead, there was a crowd. They too did the same, all of them, press themselves flat against a wall. But the horse was wild, and the cart was rocking from side to side, and a single man with his back to me was struck as the cart shuddered by. I saw it rip into his shoulder, and I heard his scream. Being a physician I ran toward him, as he fell into the street, holding his shoulder, in agony. A woman beside him began to scream for help, as I fell to the ground beside the fallen man. "I'm a doctor," I said to him, as I lay a gentle hand upon his back. "You're going to be all right." I did not know that. It's something that we always say. You know that. So I said it, as I slipped a hand down his back and slowly lowered him to the street.

You did this to me, God. This is the way that you have answered all of my years of prayer. For when I turned him from his side to his back, it was those same dark eyes looking up at me, now in terror. I pulled my shawl off, rolled it up and quickly put it beneath his head. He smiled at me weakly, upside down. I told him I had seen what had happened, and asked him how his shoulder was. He winced as he tried to move his left arm toward his right, to feel from the outside what I knew from his grimace must be very painful. Was his shoulder dislocated, broken, torn? Blood was seeping through his clothing. I was about to say something else when two servants came running through the crowd which had gathered. They were servants of his father's. But You know that. You know how they gently lifted him and carried him back to his father's house, and how I followed them. And You know how all the way there he clenched my hand and would not let go, and how each time the servants slipped or loosened their grip on him, he would shudder, wince, cry out in pain. Later, when I had examined him and found out that nothing was broken but skin, nothing dislocated but our hearts, he told me that he was ashamed that he'd cried out. And I said to him, "Every cry is a prayer." And he said, "This is the first cry of mine that has ever been answered." Surely this is a sign from You, that two men find each other who have been looking for You without success, who find You in each other. And so I say, thank you.

Al-Andalus :~

~: Toledo in Winter :~

Now that you have left that louse of a
  boyfriend and come to me
In winter when the fire behind its narrow
  grating
Barely warms us
You blame me for it not being summer
And forget all the times that I begged you to
  come here

We remain in bed till the sun is overhead
Huddled beneath blankets sewn by my
  mother and sisters
Wrapped in them when we get out of bed
Like bent old men underneath their prayer
  shawls
And we sip hot water and herbs from thick
  clay bowls
Warming our hands and laughing

And we forget all the times that you said no
   to me
Now that you are here in this cold place
Made hot by our lovemaking

So let me warm you as you warm me
And let me fill you
The way that God fills His creation
And afterwards
Wrap your arms around me
Just as God is wrapped around the world
And we will fall into sleep again in this state
   of paradox
God, immanent and transcendent
We, sinning against the Torah
While at the same time
Knowing
That what we do is holy.

Al-Andalus ∽

~: The Tutor :~

I went to the door, a loud knock interrupting my studies. He was standing alone, wrapped in a dark shawl, its fringes blown back against his cheeks, just as his hair was blown back over his brow. Had I known what I know now I would have sent him away, when he asked if I was Rabbi Elisha, the tutor. His accent was strange to me. The fire in his eyes was not. I told myself it was the fire of a young man who craves study. Oh, if only I knew then what I know now, I would have said, "No, I'm not that Rabbi Elisha."

I let him in. Never let young men in with a fire in their dark eyes, who enter your house like a thief, smiling, innocent. Had I known then what I know now I would never have opened a volume of Talmud and asked him to read. And I would never have heard that stumbling but sweet warm voice.

The world is filled with dark angels disguised as bright ones, and filled with evil lads who look like heavenly angels. He touched my forearm as I corrected him, he smiled and thanked me. Heaven knows, I have only myself to blame, as week after week he returned to study with me, and week after week I fell deeper and deeper into his net.

Fish in darkness could not have been more fooled than I, nor ended up so easily his captive. And when he said, "I have never done this before," I believed him. Had my mind only known what my body recognized, that no youth ever kissed so sweetly or so well who had never kissed before. And no young man could untied the knots in a well-knotted sash with such ease, who had never done that act before, with another man.

I have only myself to blame, for tumbling into love like a log rolled down a hill. He said he loved me, and I stopped taking the coins his uncle gave him to pay me. He said he wanted to be with me always. Fool that I am, with only myself to blame, older than he but clearly no wiser. His tutor in some things, his dog in other, following him through winding streets, wagging my tail, panting after him.

O streets of Seville, how dark and evil you are, that brought me to him unexpectedly, that lured me after him and found him, hand in hand with someone else. I could have died. I should have died. A merciful God would have taken me then, on the street, heartbroken to see that warm hand in someone else's, to see that bright smile given to another, to hear his laugh, like water tumbling over a fall. I the one who fell, over the edge into such despair.

I slinked away. He did not see me. I wept in my bed and when he came to see me the next day I tried to act as I always do, wise, older. But rage raced through me and I bellowed in pain. And when he said, "That was just a friend," how could I believe him, when the last thing I saw before I fled was those sweet lips turning toward another face?

Had I known then what I know now, the evil ways of beautiful young men, I would never have let him in, and if I did, I would never have let him touch my arm. And if I did, I would never have let him kiss me. And if I did, I would never have let him slip his hand into my robe, and untie my crimson sash. But I did. And now he is with another. Who tastes those lips, that flesh. Bad as it was to be with him, worse it is to have been with him, and to have sent him away.

Al-Andalus :~

~: The Dreamer and the Dream :~

On Friday night
I see him by himself
Eyes closed
Swaying as he chants

A week later
I see him again at Arvit
There to welcome the Sabbath
And after our prayers
He smiles as he walks past me

In the dream
He and I are walking in a lush garden
Through whose arches we can see
A beautiful city
The kind of beautiful city
That only happens in dreams

~: :~

He walks ahead of me
Leaving the garden
To enter a dimly lit library
Where I find him bent over a volume

Not wanting to disturb him
I stand behind him
Silent
Till he turns and says
"Kiss me."
I do

And wake to the taste and feel
Of his soft lips

Last night
After welcoming the Sabbath
He came up to me
Said hello
Chatted
And when he left
He kissed me
Quickly and lightly
On my left cheek

I do not know his name
Or where he lives
It is Sunday now

Al-Andalus :~

All week I must wait
For the Sabbath to return
To see if he will approach me
In the house of prayer
Come up to me again
To ask if I want to go
Walking with him

If he doesn't
Approach me
I will go up to him

Al-Andalus :~

⁊: **The Street of Butchers** ⁊~

If you walk the winding street of those who sell their bodies, women and boys, the boys more beautiful than most of the women, who are older and weary, there you will see face after hungry face, looming, offering. Three alleys away, around the bend, past the fountain – you know the way – you come upon the street of the butchers. Hanging on hooks, skinned carcasses, fly-covered, dripping with blood, are sheep and goats, their heads on the ground beneath them, staring up at you. And their empty lifeless eyes, large and dark, looming, offering, are just the same as those that extend from windows, that come at you from doorways.

Two streets, three alleys apart. The dark underbelly of our human lives. I walk the one, on hungry nights, I walk the other, on hungry days. Two streets, three alleys away. Yet one thing connects them, in the life of our bodies, the life of bodies, the God-given life of the flesh. At the far end of the butcher's street, on the left, the second stall from the end, there is a tiny hole in the wall, owned by a man named Nahshon. Apron drenched with blood, hands bloody, so long bloody that beneath his nails, no matter how long he scrubs them, dark half-circles are always found, like new moons which give off no light. But Nahshon, Nahshon is luminous. The light in his eyes, the radiance in his smile, when he sees me coming toward me. "Rabbi," he always says, smiling and bowing. I knew his father, his father knew mine, and of all the shochets in the city, he is the one most trusted by my family. But that is not why I visit him, why I order this and that cut, all sent later to my kitchen. I come to visit him because of the light. In the darkness of the quarter, bloody and dark and filled with pain, Nahshon is a star and I am one of the planets that orbit him. Nahshon is the light of God that we praise each morning.

His beard is dark, his eyes are light, his skin is dark, his soul is light. His arms are thick and hairy. His forearms swell as he lifts cleaver, as it cuts right through my heart. "This is a good cut," he says. "And I saved something for you. I expected you yesterday." Yesterday I said to myself, "Fight this. You can win." But today I said to myself, "At the sea, after we crossed it, Moses called God a warrior. This is the sea that I must cross, this sea of blood and hunger, this bloody quarter of the city, where light lives, light that warms my wet and weary soul.

Al-Andalus :~

~: While Praying :~

Women, the Talmud tells us, are a distraction. Their voices must not be heard in synagogue. And on the street, they must walk behind us, so as not to distract us again. None of those rabbis ever seem to have considered what a man's voice might do to certain women, nor did they consider how a wife must feel, walking behind her husband, always second, and yet perhaps enjoying the view. And why did they not consider this, in all of their reported wisdom, reported by themselves, it seems to me – what a room full of men praying together might do to a man like me? Did they have no one like Ishmael in Jabneh or Tiberias, in Sura or in Pumbedita, so sexy that the pillars in our prayer hall all bend toward him? To pray beside him is to pray for only one thing, him. To pray in front of him is equally to suffer, for his voice comes from somewhere so deep in his chest that anyone around him is touched in the same place, the heart, and cannot help but yearn for him. But to pray behind him in the worst of all, or the best, depending on whether you are following the rabbis' dictates or following the inclination set in your heart by God. Standing behind him, trying to focus on the "Shema" or on the "Shmoneh Esreh," those shoulders swelling, the dark hair on the back of his neck catching on his collar, the broad expanse of his back, and the way that his buttocks fill out his robe, it takes all my strength to not reach out. How can I pray, when the swell of his behind against his robe enflames my deepest desires? This, dear ancient rabbis, is enough to make a man mad, praying with Ishmael ibn Attar on a festival, or on the Sabbath. But to pray with him on Yom Kippur, or the Ninth of Av, that is like being cast down to the depths of hell at the very same time as I am tossed up to the highest heaven by burly angels. How can I be repentant, how can I be pious or solemn or feel sorrow, when an aching pain of the sweetest joy imaginable fills my body and makes me want to hide, from God, and from anyone who might see the swelling in front of my own garments? It would be better for a man like me to be banished to the women's loft above us, where behind gratings and curtains I could not see the men swaying below. No temptation for me upstairs. No Ishmael to drive me mad. Or are all of those women leaning down, straining to see him too? He is like Joseph. In one midrash I remember it says that the women of Egypt would run along the tops of walls when he went out in the streets, chasing after him, just to see his beauty. And they would throw their bracelets and rings and beads down on him, to catch his attention, to attract and reward him, simply for being beautiful. No, to sit above would not be any better for me. Worse, I would have to strain to see what I can down here so easily see. While down below, in front, beside, behind me, he is close and he is mine to lust after. "How good and pleasing it is," we sing, "for brothers to sit together." Unlike the rabbis, who did not understand these things, whoever wrote those words must have prayed with men like Ishmael.

Al-Andalus :~

~: The Rabbi's Dilemma :~

It was just after dawn on a Sabbath morning, in the years just before the Expulsion, but when already the troubles had escalated beyond tolerance. The house was silent, everyone else still in bed, when an angel appeared to the greatest rabbi in all of Spain, while he was sitting at a large wooden table, bent over a torah scroll, studying the portion of the week.

"Take pen in hand," the angel said to him, "and write down these words of God, who has sent me to you."

The rabbi, a master of Kabbalah, well versed in all the books of the Zohar, was not in the least startled to find a radiant angel standing before him, but its message, to write on the Sabbath, that puzzled him. "Perhaps," he said to himself, "this isn't really an angel at all, but a demon disguised as an angel, to tempt me and lead me astray." So he recited a particular prayer, one certain to send demons scurrying away like frightened mice. But rather than flee, the angel, for so he was now certain it must be, joined him in the prayer, the two of them saying it together, word by word. And when the prayer was done the angel repeated exactly what it had said to him the first time. "Take pen in hand, and write down these words of God, who has sent me to you."

The rabbi's mind was racing. He thought of all the situations in which it was acceptable to violate the Sabbath, all of them concerned with saving a life, but this situation did not seem to apply. Then, for he lived in an age of skeptics, when even members of his own family no longer kept the Sabbath, he considered the angel's proposition from a different angle. But he could find in himself no justification for doing what this angel had told him to do. No, the rabbi could not violate the Sabbath, although an open writing book lay in the far corner of his desk, beside a short reed pen, and a squat brass inkwell, given to him on his last birthday by his Judah, his beloved companion. For years he'd wrestled with the prohibitions on men lying with other men, and made peace with them. The ban, he and Judah agreed, forbade them certain acts which they did not commit. But keeping the Sabbath was in the Ten Commandments, and violating it was an entirely different matter to him.

"Take pen in hand," the angel said to him a third time, as he sat staring at his newly cut quill pen, "and

Al-Andalus ∻

write down these words of God, who has sent me to you."

The rabbi began to tremble. "Why is this happening to me?" he wondered. He thought to wake Judah and ask for his good counsel, as he had done many many times during the years of their long and tender union. But he was frozen in his chair, eyes cast down, looking away from the blinding light the angel cast into the room.

Back and forth the rabbi went. "I will write. I won't." Back and forth his mind went, from reasons why he should to reasons why he shouldn't. And then at last a surge of energy rose up in him, his will to do right as a Jew, in the best ways that he could, to follow this law that was given to Moses in the Ten Commandments, those ten to him more binding than all the others.

The angel must have sensed the firmness of the rabbi's decision to not write, for without him ever saying a word to it, and without it saying anything else to him, the angel vanished, just as miraculously as it had appeared. And it did not come back again.

For the rest of his life the rabbi wondered what might have happened if he had taken up the reed pen that Judah had given him, on that dark night in the very heart of Spain. Would the world have changed? Would the messiah have appeared? Would everything have turned out differently for him and for his people?

Al-Andalus :~

~: In the Domed Hall :~

For days in advance their host and all of his household cleaned and worked on the decorations. The domed hall was garlanded with grape vines and branches of juniper twined together, vines for one and juniper for the other, draped round the room and trailing in all the corners. Night and day the servants in the kitchen prepared, as they would for any other great feast, for New Year, Purim, Passover, a birth, a brit milah, a bar mitzvah, or for any wedding celebration. But in any other wedding the groom and bride would be marched through the streets by their families and friends and wed beneath the stars, in the broad open square in front of the great synagogue, while this was to be a very private wedding, an indoor wedding, a secret wedding.

Rabbi Nathan wrote the ketubah, slowly dipping pen in ink, each letter of his text building a new world. And then he decorated the wedding document with twined grape and juniper branches, just as the domed hall was being decorated.

In the marketplace, in whispers, men leaned close to talk about it. In the bathhouse, the hall of prayer, the study house, men turned to each other with knowing eyes and asked, "Have you heard about Joseph and Abner?" On the Street of Butchers, the Street of Tailors, men who knew each other and knew the two of them would stop and talk about it. "Never before, not in all of Israel!" Saul said to Beriah. "You don't know that," Beriah answered. "Perhaps before, perhaps in other times, men who loved each other did this." And in the barracks, the stables, out in the orchards, the groves, the fields, men who knew the grooms, who had been invited, stopped to talk about it, leaning on shovels, bent over furrows, paused on ladders side by side, picking olives, figs, or dates.

So the night came, a warm clear Tuesday night in early spring. The great domed hall in the home of Jacob ibn Daud, whose ancestors arrived in Spain in the time of the Roman emperors, that great domed hall, garlanded and lit with hundreds of candles, its walls ringed with tables of flowers and platters of sweets and decanters of choice wine, that great domed hall was ready to receive its guests. They arrived on horse, by foot, singly, in groups, in pairs. They took off their cloaks and shawls and entered the large domed hall, amazed by its beauty. Two flute players and two men with ouds entertained them. As they talked and laughed and waited.

Then the room fell silent, as Abner entered from the east, wearing a gold embroidered robe, with a dark red sash. And Joseph came in from the west, dressed in silver with a deep blue sash. They met beneath a white canopy, their white turbans and white prayer shawls shining in the light of all of those candles. The fringed canopy was held above their heads by two of their friends, and by Abner's cousin Daniel and Joseph's brother Judah, the one who had first introduced them, seven years before.

In a rousing voice Rabbi Isaac called out the opening words of the ceremony: "Serve God with joy, come before Him with exulting. He who is mighty, blessed and great above all beings, may He bless these two grooms." Then he raised high a wine glass, blessed the wine, and said, in words the grooms had written themselves, "And now tonight, two whose very coming together has been called an abomination, stand beneath a marriage canopy, to be united in the presence of God."

Abner took off his prayer shawl, and Joseph took off his. They kissed the ends of the neckpieces and draped them around each other. "Behold," they said together, "we are consecrated to each other by the exchange of these shawls, just as Jonathan and

David were consecrated to each other by the exchange of their cloaks." Tears were streaming down their cheeks, the rabbi's cheeks, the cheeks of everyone gathered in that large domed hall. Slowly, the rabbi read their ketubah. "Blessed are You, O Lord our God, King of the universe, who has created all things to Your glory. Blessed are You, O Lord our God, King of the universe, who has made man in your image, after your likeness." Then he read the end of their marriage contract, which concluded with David and Jonathan's words, from the Book of Samuel. "As for the promise we made to each other, may God be between you and me forever."

No wine glass was broken at that celebration. "Too much is broken in our lives already," the rabbi said, as he handed a golden cup to Abner and Joseph to drink from. Then he passed the shining cup around the room so that all the men gathered there could sip from it. When it had circled the room and come back to him, the rabbi wrapped that marriage cup in cloth of gold and placed it in a carved wooden box with two angels on top of it. "As a sign and seal of your union," he said to the two grooms. Then Abner, so tall and dark, leaned down to kiss Joseph, his beloved, so fair. And everyone in that blazing hall cheered and wished them well.

Then the rabbi turned to their assembled guests and said, "Tonight in darkness, in secrecy, but next year, out in the square before the great synagogue. Tonight in this domed hall, decorated with twined branches of grape and juniper. But next year beneath the firmament of heaven, decorated by the sun and its golden rays. Tonight we are enslaved by old laws. But next year we will be free."

And they danced the night away, men and men, women and women, women and men, in each other's arms, laughing and crying from joy. In Spain, right before the feast of Passover, sheltered by that great domed hall, draped with twined juniper and grape vines.

Al-Andalus :~

~: Before the Expulsion :~

The rabbis of Toledo hated my Uncle Alvaro almost as much as I do, to this very day. My mother's only brother was a rich man, a merchant of silver and gold, but that was not why the rabbis hated him. He was also a scholar, well versed in the ancient and little read poetry of ibn Gabirol, HaLevi, and ibn Ezra, but that is not why the rabbis hated him either. And Alvaro da Luna was a poet himself, but it was not for his poems alone that the rabbis hated him, or why I hate him, his unforgiving namesake.

Let me be honest here. My uncle's poems were second-rate imitations, written in the style of the poets he adored. Those poets were among the jewels of our glorious past. Their prayers became our words when we cried out to God on Sabbath and holidays, which we did with increasing frequency in that time before our exile. But those were not the writings that my uncle imitated and shared with his friends. No, the poems he favored were the ones that our noble poets had written to beautiful young men. Those poems our rabbis chose to ignore. But it was because of those poems, and his own, that the rabbis of Toledo, and all of Spain, came to hate my uncle.

Once Don Isaac, an elder of our beleaguered community, came to visit my father. He sat pale and in tears at our table, his gnarled hands stretched out, imploring. "Don Fernando my friend, when Koran and Gospel agree with the Torah about a particular sin, surely God is speaking to us all." I remember those words to this day, sitting in my dusty room in Salonika. And I remember the pained look on my father's face. For there were continued hostilities between Jews and *conversos*, between *conversos* and the church, and given the increasing power of the Inquisition, and the lack of support for us from their Most Catholic Majesties Ferdinand and Isabella, my uncle's life was a danger to us all.

Had my uncle been just a poet, the rabbis would not have hated him quite so much. And had he been guilty only of carnal relations with beautiful young men, no one would have been the wiser, for many men did that, in baths and taverns – even rabbis, I am told. But what angered the rabbis and elders of our city was that my uncle won the favors of one young man after another, and was seen with them in public, his arms around them, entwined, caressing.

Al-Andalus ∿

The very evening of Don Isaac's visit, my father went to my uncle's house, at the opposite end of the quarter, near the Gate of the Jews. My mother and I waited for him in the lower hall. Not a single word did Father speak upon his return, but from his silence we knew the visit had been a failure. The Jewish quarter had been under a state of attack for almost a hundred years. My uncle had given great sums to repair the walls, to rebuild burned synagogues, and could always be counted on to help families in need. It was his largesse, I suppose, that made him feel above the law, and above common sense in such dangerous times.

One day, not long after Don Isaac's visit, the cook ran out of saffron for our Sabbath pot of *adafina*. Those were the sorts of purchases my mother liked to make herself. But when we went out, to shop, to pray, people would glare and point at us, or turn away, to whisper, to snicker. So we'd been staying home as much as possible. But my sisters were tired of being trapped indoors, and begged Mother to let us all go out. We set out first thing in the morning, hoping the streets would be empty, and made our way quickly up the Calle de la Judería to the market, then straight to the stall of Mother's favorite spice vendor. She was bent over spice baskets when my older sister Beatriz nudged my younger sister Graça and pointed her head toward a young man standing behind us. "Look at his lashes," she whispered, loud enough for me to hear her.

Curious, I turned myself, to see a tall broad shouldered young man a few years older than I was, standing in profile at the stall across from us, looking at brass hanging lamps. His lashes were long, like the dark wings of a bird caressing his cheeks, long and dark enough to make any girl jealous. For he was beautiful like a girl, and yet manly at the same time, with his new young beard growing down from flared cheekbones, like the roots of a sapling spreading deep into the earth.

As people often do when someone is staring at them, this handsome young man felt our eyes upon him, and turned to look back at us. My sisters, now terrified, darted in front of our mother, who was haggling with the spice seller. And he and I found ourselves gazing at each other.

His eyes were dark and deep, like two pools in a courtyard, side by side, like two great night seas, of just the black light mystics write about, the black light that existed before anything else was created. And for a moment I felt as if there were something solid cast between the depths of his eyes and mine, vines, ropes, chains of brass like the ones on the hanging lamps he had turned away from. Ropes, chains, arms reaching out in supplication. But then, frightened myself, I too turned away, not to hide

Al-Andalus ∾

in front of Mother, but to look at spices, casually, calmly, my heart beating furiously beneath my white fringed cloak.

For days I was haunted by the image of that young man, his darks eyes staring down into my heart whenever my own eyes were closed. Like a weed that grows tall in your garden, he had taken up residence in my mind, broad and strong. I had never seen him before, but kept going back to the market whenever I had a chance, hoping that I would see him again. But I never did.

Several weeks later my uncle invited me to his house, to hear some of his new poems. Father did not want me to go, but Mother was afraid to offend him. After much discussion they asked Gedaliah, one of our old servants, to accompany me. I was nervous as we walked the familiar route to Uncle Alvaro's house. I was trembling when one of my uncle's servants let us in. And to this day I can remember how startled I was when I entered the large room beyond the courtyard, the painted room where my uncle received friends and family. For there was the young man with the beautiful eyes, sprawled on cushions, beside a round brass table. A single garnet set in gold caught the light as he reached a long slim hand toward a plate of almonds and *biscochos* that sat near the table's edge. Tossing his shining dark hair back, he looked up at me and smiled. I knew from that smile that he did not remember me.

Later the two of them must have laughed, laughed at how awkward I was, how I stammered and stuttered and left the house quickly, the moment that Uncle Alvaro finished reading his poems. Or were they pained by my behavior? I have wondered that too. Did they think my spilling wine and dropping almonds on the cool tile floor as my uncle read was a sign of my disapproval or disgust? That I felt tainted by them, like a hungry man who in desperation eats pork or rabbit meat, but then hates himself?

I never knew how my uncle met Joseph, his beloved, Joseph of the beautiful eyes. Perhaps it was in the very same market where I had first seen him. Rumor had it that Uncle Alvaro paid Joseph's family a large sum of money to give their son up to him, which they gladly did, for they were poor, a family of cobblers, or so our servants said.

And now I have grandsons who are Joseph's age, the age that I was when we were forced to leave our ancient home. We fled east to Salonika, where my father's younger brother Solomon lived. Alvaro and his beloved fled south, to Tangiers, where my uncle had extensive trade connections. Unlike the succession of young men that came and went before him, Joseph remained with my uncle. Both of them are dead now. So much is dead. I wear around my neck

Al-Andalus :~

the key to our house in Toledo. My father wore it until the day he died, and when I die it will pass to Ephraim, my eldest son. But beneath that key lie the ropes that still bind me to those bottomless eyes, and to the memory of my uncle's coarse thick hairy hand, reaching out to stroke Joseph's soft dark cheek. Joseph, who is beauty, who is Spain, who is everything lost to us.

And you wonder why I hate my uncle, from half a world away, and all these long years later.

Avodah

∽: DIVINE SERVICE :∼

Avodah :~

~: Shacharit :~
Light in the Tree

A UPS man brought the carton right to their door. Inside the carton was a small square blue footlocker, and inside the footlocker, in a Styrofoam shell, sat a squat round metal thermos. Vapor rose up from it as Sara and Rachel unscrewed the top, from the liquid nitrogen the vials of sperm were hanging in, which came from a donor clinic in New York City that only worked with Jewish men. For four months in a row, each time the carton came, they would burn incense, light candles, play soft music, and carefully follow the instructions Louisa their gynecologist gave them. Each night in bed Sara and Rachel, would sing their favorite songs to their future baby. But when Sara's period came for the fourth month in a row, they lit a blue candle to give thanks and say good-bye to Number 658, the semi-anonymous donor they'd chosen from piles of folders the clinic sent them, a thirty-eight year old kayak enthusiast with a Ph.D. in philosophy, who taught at a women's college back East.

Rachel, a tall lanky woman with short-cropped dark hair, was a senior editor at a large publishing company in San Francisco. She specialized in children's books, and had written, illustrated, and published two of her own. Sara, short and round with spiky red hair, was an acupuncturist and massage therapist who worked at a small holistic health center whose clients were mainly men with HIV and AIDS. They met at their friends' Kelly and Marissa's commitment ceremony, and after five years together they were ready to start a family. Because they couldn't afford anything in the city, they bought a 1960's ranch house on a quiet street across the bay in Albany, with three bedrooms and a large sunny backyard. They still got together with their friends in the city, and the commute wasn't that bad. Rachel had painted a border of alternating orange rabbits and purple giraffes on the wall of one of the bedrooms, and all that was missing in their lives was a baby to inhabit that small sunny room. So they pulled out the stack of folders from the clinic and eventually agreed on Donor 498, an architect who specialized in low-income housing and was also a former child prodigy on the piano.

They had great hopes for 498, but after Sara got her fourth period, they went back to Louisa, who ran a series of tests which all came back saying that Sara was in excellent health. "Sometimes," Louisa said, "the process can become stressful. Why don't you take a break for a few months, before you start again?" Over dinner in the kitchen that Friday night, with candles flickering in Sara's Grandma Sophie's silver sabbath candlesticks, they discussed Sara taking a leave of absence from her job, expecting that she would soon be pregnant with Donor 537. He was a gay software designer with two brothers and a sister, who played tennis, ran marathons and used to be an aerobics instructor, all of which sounded excessively healthy to them, and perfect for the father of their child.

The first day she was at home, after Rachel went off to work, Sara wandered out to the yard in her bathrobe. Sipping a cup of chamomile tea, she sat on the grass, listening to the water gurgling in the artificial stream. She did the same thing the next day. After a week of that Rachel said over dinner, "You look so relaxed, honey. Keep this up and you'll be preggers in no time." They let go of Rosaria, the cleaning woman who came in once a week, and Sara started taking care of the house. When she was still working they'd eaten out most nights, or picked up takeout, but Sara started cooking and Rachel found to her delight (and Sara's) that she liked coming home to her every evening, liked what Sara cooked, and liked having her do the laundry. "It must be some old patriarchal gene," she said, jokingly, as both of their mothers worked when they were growing up, and still worked. "Some deep animal desire for a femmy wife slaving over a hot stove."

Each morning, while Rachel showered and dressed, Sara would go downstairs and make breakfast. After Rachel left the house Sara would get back in bed, drifting in and out of sleep, like a cat in a sunny window, reveling in the warmth. Then, rested, she would do whatever she felt drawn to, in no particular order. She would iron for a while, wash the breakfast dishes, clean the tub, water the plants, rearrange the kitchen cabinets, dust, vacuum, although it was hard for her to go into what they called the baby's room.

"Do you think I'll go brain dead?" she asked her best friend Stephanie on the phone. They'd been college roommates at Berkeley.

"You might, if you do it for too long. But you'll be pregnant soon and then everything will be different."

"But I like housework. It's so concrete, so enduring. And way less depressing than sticking needles in someone who's sick and then sending him home, not sure that I'll ever see him again. And I can't believe what I'm about to say, Steph, but cleaning the house is like a spiritual act. A kind of meditation."

Avodah :~

Stephanie couldn't believe it either. She feared that staying at home had already gotten to Sara, but said she was happy for her. "Only, while you're waiting, why not do a few massage clients a week, at home, just to keep on your toes?"

Sara said she'd think about it. "And I'm letting my hair grow," she said, to change the subject. She did think about Stephanie's suggestion, but did nothing about it, and three months later she still wasn't pregnant, so they fired the gardener. Having grown up in an apartment in New York, Sara had never had a yard before. She went to the local bookstore and came home with a stack of gardening books that she would read in bed at night while Rachel watched television or played computer games. She was especially good at Go and Solitaire. Sara was especially interested in roses.

Working in the yard was heaven for Sara. Rather than keeping on her toes, she discovered that she loved feeling her bare feet buried deep in the earth. After reading an article in the gardening section of the paper, Sara went out and bought a bin and started a compost heap. Rachel thought that was going a bit far, but after a while she got used to the plastic container on the kitchen counter that all the food scraps went into. And she could see how well their garden was doing since Sara started shoveling out the dark rich soil from the outdoor bin. Sara had dug up a section of the lawn in the backyard and put in a small vegetable garden. She began with four rows, of lettuce, tomatoes, carrots, and summer squash, with the intention of growing more if the first season went well.

There was another lesbian couple in the neighborhood, who had two teenagers, and a few older women whose kids had gone off to college, but there was only one other woman in the neighborhood who didn't have kids and who stayed at home, a seventy-year-old widow, Mrs. Wallace. All the other women on the block worked except for her. Sara suspected that there must be other women in the neighborhood in her situation, young, at home, and childless, but she didn't know any. It seemed odd to her that what had been common two generations before and was still common in other parts of the country, was rare now, rare where they lived.

Rachel had several friends from work that she sometimes met for dinner and two that she went running with or played tennis with, but once she was at home Sara drifted away from her old friends, all of whom worked. Sometimes they'd get together with Kelly and Marissa, whose wedding they met at, but they still lived in the city, and now that they had Trevor and Kaitlin, finding time to get together was always difficult. Sensing that Sara might be lonely, Rachel suggested that they join a synagogue.

Avodah ~

On Friday nights they would dress up and check out various shuls in the area. Sara had gone to Hebrew School and had a bat mitzvah. Although she hadn't been to temple in years, she still lit candles on Friday night. Rachel's family was secular and she'd had no religious education. Rachel was surprised that she liked going to services. "The songs make me feel good." But for Sara, nothing in any of the congregations they visited came close to the serenity she experienced cleaning or gardening. And with her crops coming up, much to Rachel's delight and her own, Sara was feeling purposeful in a way that she had never felt before, so they stopped going to services.

Rachel was happy that Sara was happy. But then Stephanie called Rachel at work one day. "I'm nervous about her, Rache. She'd get that way when she was depressed. Be all sweet to cover it up. And keep busy doing mindless things." Rachel thought she knew her partner pretty well, but after Stephanie's call she began to worry. At dinner a few nights later she asked, "Honey, are you sure you're happy being at home alone all day? I mean, don't you miss going out and doing things, having lunch with friends, working with clients? I go running with Deanna and Marjorie, but you haven't made a single new friend since we moved here. And you don't see anyone from the clinic anymore."

"What about Jeanne Wallace, down the street?" Sara asked, looking up from her plate, where she had arranged a fan of steamed vegetables around a pile of wild rice and sautéed shiitake mushrooms. Jeanne was teaching Sara how to tend roses. "Did you know that Golden Gate Park was all sand dunes, less than a hundred years ago?" Sara said. "And that Silicon Valley used to be called the Valley of Heart's Delight? Jeanne told me that." Rachel paused for a moment, knife and fork poised over her plate. "But she's your grandmother's age." Sara glared at her. "What's wrong with that? Have you suddenly turned into an ageist?" Rachel put her knife and fork down, more gently than she really wanted to. "I meant nothing by it, honey. I just want to make sure you're happy. And as soon as we get pregnant, you can reconsider."

Sara assured Rachel that she *was* happy. Rachel believed her and decided she'd been silly to trust Stephanie. But as Sara lay in bed that night, listening to Rachel's soft breathing, it occurred to her that when Rachel asked if she was happy at home what she meant was that she was tired of Sara's perkiness. "What if there *is* something wrong with me? And I'm just keeping busy to cover it up. Maybe I should be on Prozac."

The next morning, after she sent Rachel off to work, instead of getting back in bed or sitting out in the garden, Sara called Ignacio, the boss at her clinic, to say that she was almost ready to come back. He said her clients all missed her, that he hoped she'd return soon. Sara said she'd think about it and call again by the end of the week. Then she went into the bathroom to play with her hair, which was now just long enough to pull back into a short ponytail. Then she went down to wash the breakfast dishes, do another load of laundry, and made herself vacuum the baby's room. She never told Rachel that she'd called Ignacio, and she never called him back.

One afternoon, in shorts and an old tee shirt, Sara was standing in the supermarket checkout line, her cart piled high with groceries, when she noticed an article on the cover of a woman's magazine. The words *How to Spice up Your Marriage* were staring at her in bold red letters, above a square yellow cake decorated with green ribbons of icing to look like a wrapped-up birthday present. Never in all her life had she picked up a tabloid or a magazine like that. Sara looked around to see if anyone was watching her, then grabbed the magazine and flipped through it till she came to the article. Just as she found it the forty-something blond cashier with a big rhinestone studded cross around her neck said to the woman in front of her, "Good bye, dear. Have a nice day!" Sara closed the magazine and was about to put it back on the rack when the cashier said to her, "Isn't that a darling cake?" Feeling like a child caught shoplifting, and amazed by the cashier's assumption about her, Sara tossed the magazine on the conveyor belt and began to unload her groceries.

Back home, after she put everything away, Sara went out to the yard with the magazine. The first paragraph of the article warned her of something that all at-home wives ought to remember. While their husbands are out in the world meeting new people and facing new challenges, their own work tends to be isolating, repetitive, and over time that could become boring for their husbands to hear about. She had no trouble turning "husband" into "partner," she was used to doing that, but the article didn't suggest ways to add excitement to her conversations with Rachel. Instead the writer, a "noted psychologist" she'd never heard of, said the best way to spice up your marriage was to come up with something you could do for yourself, something harmless and secret that would give you joy and pleasure.

The article continued on another page, and flipping to find it, Sara guessed that it would tell her to buy a tiny box of expensive chocolates, take a fancy bubble bath in the middle of the afternoon, or go out alone for a delicious lunch in a beautiful restaurant. Instead, the article suggested several different projects, such as wallpapering her closet, which seemed ridiculous to Sara, taking up needlepoint, which seemed too fussy and difficult, or learning how to play a musical instrument. Sara had taken piano lessons for three years as a young girl and been terrible at it. Besides, she and Rachel had a huge collection of CDs ranging from contemporary Jazz to Japanese music, and she couldn't imagine that Rachel would put up with her banging around for years on end on a piano or flute. She didn't much like the idea herself.

For several days Sara moped about the house, and Rachel noticed. She complimented Sara on her hair, which was down to her shoulders, wavy and red. But she was afraid to ask her about her mood, especially as they'd just started with a new donor, 488, a pediatrician who was already the donor father of three other children, which seemed a good sign. They were both waiting to see if she'd get her period, which was a tense time every month. In a sad way, once her period would come, they were both relieved. Life could go back to normal, although they'd finally discussed seeing a fertility doctor if they weren't pregnant again in three more months. Louisa had given her the name of someone she recommended, down at Stanford. But Sara, long involved in holistic health care, was resistant to beginning the regimen she knew women had to undergo, of hormones and other invasive treatments. And neither of them were ready to talk about adoption, so they continued doing what they were doing, with Donor 488.

Two days later Rachel came home with a gift-wrapped box for her, a surprise. She found Sara out in the yard, in a pair of cut-off jeans and one of her old tank tops, blazoned with the name of her old basketball team, the Slamazons, digging a pit near the artificial stream. "I'm putting in a water-lily pool," she said, looking up at Rachel over her shoulder. There was dirt on her face. Rachel found it endearing and held out the box to her, which Sara opened with utter delight, white tissue paper giving way to a tall blue cobalt glass vase. "For the roses," they both said simultaneously, which were just starting to blossom. Sara ran into the house to get a pair of scissors.

As she came out of the house she saw Rachel, her jacket off and her sleeves rolled up, standing in the pit and digging where she'd left off. Afraid to tell her that that was her special project, and annoyed that she had started to participate in it, Sara went off to cut some roses, cool her anger, and decided she would have to come up with something else.

The next morning, as soon as Rachel's car pulled out of the driveway, Sara ran into the family room and pulled out the magazine from under the pile of old unread *New Yorker*s where she'd hidden it. "Something all your own that you don't tell your husband about," she read again. "Something exciting that fills you with joy." But nothing came to her. She thought about calling Stephanie or Jeanne Wallace, who had never worked, raised three boys, and seemed like a very happy person. Yes, that was a better idea than calling Stephanie, who had been married to Skip for less than four months when she moved out, and who, since that time, had dated a succession of men she never intended to marry. Sara dialed Jeanne's number, but there was no answer. Jeanne was the only person she knew who didn't have an answering machine. "I'll try her later."

Sara went into the family room and plunked down in an overstuffed tan chair. Across from her were a large-screen television, a DVD player, and their sound system. On the coffee table in front of her was a basket filled with beach rocks she and Rachel had gathered over the years, in Baja, Santa Cruz, Mendocino, and Maui, where they went on their honeymoon. She was about to turn on a talk show but the light of late morning was coming in through the window behind her, falling on the rocks with the softest caress. Sara leaned over to look at them more closely, aware that the light had a quality she'd never seen before. There was a golden richness to it. The rocks did not seem to be illuminated by the sun. They appeared to be glowing from within.

Just then, in the olive tree in the yard behind her, whose olives Jeanne was going to show her how to cure, a single dove began to coo. Sara turned to it and noticed the same golden glow surrounding and suffusing the dove, the tree, in fact everything in the backyard. The stream that meandered through five rocks the former owners had chosen on a trip to Japan seemed to be flowing like liquid diamonds. And the rocks themselves, gray-brown and craggy, seemed to be emerging from the earth like gnarled old women, each with her own distinct personality. Sara laughed out loud. One rock seemed wise, one feisty, one sad, one a fierce crone, and the smallest one was rather like her grandmother Rose the last time she saw her in her nursing home, sweet and curled up and not quite all there.

There was a soft wind blowing up from the bay, and wisps of skittering clouds. Sara knew they came over the bay from the coast, bringing the sea along, wild and salty. It was months since she and Rachel had driven out there, and Sara realized that she missed walking by the ocean. She got up and went out into the yard, drawn by the sea smell, which seemed so far from home. Kneeling on the grass beside the stream, admiring the first water lilies coming up in her pond, she was pulled into the sound of the water, into the glorious morning sunshine that was sparkling on its surface. Leaning down to dip a hand into the stream, her long red braid dropped into the water. And she felt as if she had become a part of it. A part, not just of that small water, but a

Avodah :~

part of all waters, all streams, lakes, rivers, bays, seas, and oceans. A part too of the primal waters that God divided at the beginning of creation. Radiant as the sunlight, liquid and tingling, Sara felt vaster than she had ever imagined a person could feel.

Gradually that expansive feeling faded, and Sara picked herself up, went back into the house, and did the breakfast dishes. Then she made a marinade for the vegetables she was going to grill that night for dinner. After that, she did the laundry, three loads, and spent some time out front, pulling weeds. But even though that curious feeling was gone, and the world went back to the way it usually seemed, something of its radiance remained. And when Rachel got home from the gym that night, she danced Sara around the kitchen, instinctively responding to her happiness.

Over the next few days, without her trying to summon it, light or sound or a smell would trigger that feeling again. Once it happened while she was watching their clothes spinning in the dryer. Then it happened when she was walking by the baby's room and noticed a shaft of light angling in through the half-closed wooden blinds. She went in and sat on the floor for the first time, bathed in golden beauty. A few days later it happened again when she was sitting in the driveway pulling weeds from a patch of grass edged with lavender and brilliant orange poppies. The poppies, and each blade of grass, were stretching up to the sun like worshippers in rapt devotion. All of them part of a vast, exalting oneness, reminding her of the words from a morning prayer, that God renews the work of creation every day.

Sara had forgotten all about the article, but sitting in the driveway that morning, it came back to her. She realized that her experience was everything the article had talked about. It was exciting and filled her with joy. She thought about telling Rachel, but the article said that it was something for her to keep to herself. Yes, this would be her own little secret. Better than chocolates or having a secret affair. Sprawled out in the bright morning sun. Listening to the ivy growing up the side of the house, singing its way toward the warm shingled roof, with utter delight in just being alive.

~: **Musaf** :~
Pink Izzy

It has been two years since Isidore Isaac Berman died. Several months before his death he completed the manuscript of his collected poems. When his publisher asked me to write an introduction, I was hesitant. So much has been written about Pink Izzy, the war hero. But that isn't what they wanted. They wanted me to say something about the man who wrote the poems.

I remember the day that I met Colonel Berman. A gawky man of twenty-six, sleeves rolled up, in a makeshift uniform, he was running his post from a bunker in the subway under 14th Street. I had raced uptown on my bicycle, from the fort at the Battery where I was stationed, carrying a message from General Eisenhower. I was nineteen years old, and had no idea as I peddled through barricades, over rubble, that this was a day that would change my life.

It was May 19th, 1944. Washington had fallen to the Nazis in April, just as Paris, London and Moscow had fallen before it. Peking and New Delhi had fallen to the Japanese. Congress and the president had retreated, first to St. Louis and then to Denver, midway between the attack zones of the Germans on the east and the Japanese on the west. One by one all the cities on both coasts had fallen, except for New York and the area around it.

The residents of Manhattan who hadn't fled were at the point of starvation, and were under constant air attack from German aircraft carriers in the harbor. Our only hope had been that the government in Denver would send troops to support us, but the Germans cut them off whenever they tried to cross the Mississippi.

I knew the end was near. I'd barely made it north. Found Colonel Berman, known to everyone since childhood as Pink Izzy, for his strawberry red hair and florid complexion, in the 14th Street bunker, behind a wall of sandbags, a single electric light bulb flickering. Silent, he read the general's message, in the little room he camped out in, in the rubble of the subway, in what used to be a newspaper stand. He lit a kerosene lamp. Put his rifle down. Closed the flimsy door behind us. Pointed me to a chair. Then he unstrapped his ammo pack, and sat down at his desk to compose a message for me to take back to General Eisenhower.

Avodah ~

To this day I can hear the sound of his pen scratching on paper, how he put it down, sighed – and then everything I had been holding back burst out of me. I began to sob, and he stood up, came toward me. Tears were streaming down his face, as he reached his hands out and put them on my shoulders. In the distance, the bombs started again. I did not hear them. All I heard was the beating of his heart. And what seemed like hours later, when he went back to his desk, I thought that he was finishing his message, but instead he was beginning his most famous poem, the one they read in High School English classes, along with Dickinson and Whitman, "The Bombs Were Falling on His Kisses."

When the bombing stopped, we emerged from the rubble to a cloudless day whose sky was jagged. That tower of strength, built by my father, my uncles, my older brothers, the tallest building in the world, the Empire State Building, was bombed to half its height. And looking south, the island was now flat almost all the way to Wall Street. Pointing, he said, "My family..." I took his trembling hand. There was nothing I could say. And no way for me to get back to the Battery. Izzy and his communications officer struggled to find a working band. But there was only static. It was then that Izzy ordered all his soldiers to flee the island through the tunnels under the Hudson. When we were all across we bombed them so that the Germans could not use them.

Hours later, in the dark, we arrived in Newark, on foot. Swarms of soldiers followed us, civilians, messengers. By the time we got there, Izzy knew that Eisenhower was dead, that the Denver government had surrendered, and that he was probably the highest-ranking free officer in German Occupied Territory. We passed the night in a large house on the outskirts of the city. It was there, in that old suburban house, that Izzy wrote "I Took His Hand in Darkness." I carried that poem in my wallet for the rest of the war. The paper finally came apart along the folds, but I continued to carry it. I carry it still.

The two of us lay holding each other all through the night. We did not sleep. We did not speak. We never undressed. Just before dawn, Izzy roused his men and we fled. West to the woods, going deeper and deeper toward safety, beginning a seven-year journey that would take us up and down the German East Coast into the Free States to meet with the government in Denver, making forays into Japanese Occupied Territory, attacking, retreating, and then vanishing. Often we slept in the woods, in snow, in rain. The Germans and Japanese wanted us, searched for us. But we moved from place to place along a new Underground Railroad, patterned on memories of the one that had moved escaping slaves up north and into freedom before and during the Civil War. That was the last war on our soil. Who could imagine that less than one hundred years later, there would be fighting on American soil again? Not a war between the states, but an invasion.

During the next night, across the border in Pennsylvania, having requisitioned cars and trucks from farmers and townspeople, Izzy began to organize the resistance movement that would contribute to the defeat of the Axis powers in America. And it was on that night, our third night together, that Colonel Isidore Berman, Jew, and his assistant, Private First Class Jonny Strongfeather, Mohawk, in the attic of an abandoned farm house, consummated their marriage.

Izzy grew up in a tenement in the Lower East Side. I grew up in a shack on a reservation in upstate New York. Our worlds were different and our paths would never have crossed had it not been for the war. But from that night till the night he died, forty-one years later, Izzy and I were never apart. I don't know how many of the people around us knew that we were lovers. There was too much else to think about. Of course, rumors got back to us, and I remember the day when Izzy decided that we didn't have to deny them. "Red," (that was what he called me, not from the color of my hair, he called us "Pink and Red,") "what if we just tell the truth? Half the guys out there are doing the same thing. And if we're fighting for our lives, isn't this a part of what we're fighting for?" And in every place we came to, workers and farmers and townfolk defied the occupation forces, stepped beyond their old moralities, and worked with us for freedom. As if they remembered that there had been a time, when the land belonged to my ancestors, that men like us were honored and considered holy.

In the first years after the Partition, we began to hear rumors about resettlement camps for Jews and Chinese and Africans and Gypsies and Indians. People told us that inmates were being used in experiments, worked to death, or simply killed, just as the Nazis had already done in Central Europe, then in England and North Africa, and the Japanese in China, India, and Southeast Asia.

Everyone knows the public Pink Izzy, that jaunty man with wild red hair and crooked glasses, the resistance hero. There are scores of books about his war years. But none of them mention how he sobbed, leading his forces through the gates of the Narrowsburg death camp, through the feeble outstretched arms of those we came to liberate. Or his horror, walking through the large immaculate white-tiled "Elimination Chambers," where the Nazis had perfected their killing and vaporization techniques, rendering murder stainless and nearly invisible. And when they quote from my favorite poem of his, "Very and Red," they remember that after the war it helped to persuade the representatives of Congress in Denver to grant the American Indians our own land and full autonomy. Without our labor as runners and spies, using our own languages to create codes neither the Germans nor Japanese could break, we would never have been able to defeat Chancellor Rommel, Viceroy Tojo and the combined Axis forces. But none of them know that he wrote it the day we found out that the last group of East Coast Indians had died in a "resettlement" camp in Pennsylvania.

In January of 1948, we were hiding out in a small house near Atlanta, Georgia, still under German control. Our hosts were a Jewish family who had survived with forged identity papers. Our hostess, Mrs. Gilman, used up two weeks of ration coupons to prepare a feast. I could feel Izzy tremble and then control himself, when he saw the little bow-tie noodles on his plate, a favorite of his family when he was a boy.

Later that night, we sat down to watch the first television program most of us had ever seen. Televisions were beginning to be found in American homes all over German Overseas America. It was only later that we found out that that brilliant tool for propaganda, run by the filmmaker Leni Riefenstahl, came to us on sets manufactured in concentration camps. The Gilmans had a set, tuned to the English language station and we all huddled around it in their crowded living room, illuminated by its flickering light. The news came on. Behind the commentator was a large familiar map of America divided in thirds, the east for the Germans and west for the Japanese, with a strip in the middle that remained the Free States.

I was sitting next to Izzy and I could feel how tightly he was gripping the arm of the couch. When that program was over, we all went back to our makeshift beds. Izzy sat up with a candle, writing the first verses of what would become "America the Beautiless." The bomb filled skies, the blackened waves of grain, the burning mountains. It was the juxtaposition of the meal and the map of a country that no longer stretched from "sea to shining sea" that triggered the poem, although those images don't appear in the final version.

Even today, decades later, we drive through the rubble of towns and cities, see downed planes in the middle of corn fields, stop to pray at the monuments to the dead that were erected on every American Main Street. Is there anyone in this country who has not lost a friend, a relative, a neighbor? And had the Australians not invented the atomic bomb, and dropped it on Berlin and Tokyo on New Years Day

Avodah ∼

of 1950, this country would still be divided in three, Izzy and I and all the others like us would have died long ago in the camps, this book would be but a hazy dream from a parallel universe.

When the city of Washington was recaptured in November of 1950, Izzy spent four days in the German Military High command in Virginia, searching through records looking for the imprisonment and death records of our families. Those nights, he would come back to our camp a broken man. As broken when he found my family's records as he was when he found his own. But somehow each morning he would put himself together again so that his soldiers, who loved him, would be inspired to duty without revenge, and healing without recrimination. In Europe they killed collaborators, they killed Germans, but except for a few scattered incidents, that never happened in America, because of Izzy's stern directives and his troops' example. After the war a woman in Seattle sent us a carbon copy of his poem, "Now Living Together in Peace," that Izzy had given to a resistance officer in Chicago, who passed it from hand to hand till it got to her.

I am sitting at Izzy's desk now, as I write, looking up at a framed copy of the famous *Life* magazine cover, of President Roosevelt standing in front of the Capital Building in Denver, pinning a medal of honor on Izzy's uniform, for his valor as head of the American resistance movement. Izzy is looking down at his shoes, and the president is flashing her toothy smile, so familiar to us since 1945 when her husband died in Denver and she took the helm of our divided nation.

That is a moment in history. The Second Great War was over. The Axis powers had been defeated. But I also remember another moment. Several years later Izzy and I went to the opening night of the movie made about his life. We laughed at the two handsome actors who portrayed us, a funny looking Jew and an equally funny looking Indian. During the war scenes, the man who mobilized tens of thousands of Americans, who liberated the death camps in Pennsylvania, New York and Virginia, sat with his eyes closed, clutching my hand. He was shaking as we watched those two dashing men on March 24th, 1951, when the officers of the German High Command surrendered to him in the lobby of an old theatre in Louisville, Kentucky. And he laughed at the re-creation of the medal award, at ourselves and the too pretty actress playing President Roosevelt. Cried at the end as long lines of prisoners marched by, wearing their identification badges: A red circle for Indians, black diamond for Negroes, the yellow star for Jews, the yellow square for Chinese, and green P for political prisoners. And of course, the pink triangle reserved for men like us. Each verse of

Avodah :~

"The Colors of Death," Izzy's long poem about the liberation of the camps, begins with a description of another one of those badges. Till the day he died, he wore a jacket with all of them sewn on it.

After the war, Izzy and I returned to New York. We found an apartment on the East Side, in a neighborhood that hadn't been bombed. The day that we moved in he nailed a dead bullet casing to our doorframe. When I asked him about it he told me that it was there instead of a mezuzah, that small box with prayers in it that Jews nail to the doorposts of their homes.

It was like moving through a dream to be back there. A short walk from our apartment would take us from old familiar streets to unrecognizable neighborhoods around the corner, built by the Germans during the Occupation. I remember the Victory Parade. There was no Wall Street or Broadway to march up as Lindbergh had once done. No ticker tape pouring down like snow. We marched up the new Goethe Boulevard, to screaming cheers. And when a woman broke out of the crowd and leaped at our car, Izzy grabbed her up in his arms. It his only remaining relative, Aunt Frances, who survived the war hiding in the mountains of upstate New York. Frances became our family, welcoming us as a couple in a way that would never have happened before the war.

We never moved from that apartment. From our bedroom window on 33rd Street you can see the jagged top of the Empire State Building, cut off at the sixty-fifth floor. It has never been rebuilt, but is still the tallest building in new New York, a memorial. We stopped there a few months before Izzy died of the cancer he had been battling for several years, on a long slow walk through Manhattan. The sky was clear, and it was early spring.

We stopped where Macy's used to be, where Izzy had his first job, as a thirteen-year-old, in the stockrooms. We stopped where the Chrysler Building used to be. We stopped where the Metropolitan Opera used to be. We visited the site of Grand Central Station, and delighted in glorious light-flooded Pennsylvania Station, patterned after some ancient Roman baths, he told me, one of the few old Midtown buildings which remains. Sometimes we could not find the exact locations of old places, beneath the new structures the Germans built, and the ones that we built after the war. We tried to remember where they were and what they looked like. Sitting in a luncheonette on Colorado Avenue, Izzy took out a little pad he always kept in his jacket pocket, and wrote "The Lights of Early Afternoon." The poem begins in Ohio, where we were waiting for a German convoy, and Izzy had stopped and knelt down in the grass at the side of the road, to smell the lily-of-the-val-

Avodah ⁖

ley that had just begun to blossom. In a small house beside the road, a radio was playing, softly. We could hear the voice of President Roosevelt on Radio Free America, calling on us to continue in our struggles. The poem goes back and forth from the flowers to her voice to the knowledge that in fifteen minutes ten German trucks will be passing by, and all of their soldiers will be dead in our ambush. The poem ends with the color of the sky, the smell of the flowers, the voice of reasoned hope, the light streaming through glass above us in the station.

On the way home from the parade we stopped at 14th Street to visit the place where we met. The new subway station is immaculate, and except for a plaque that announces it, you would never know that a war had been fought in and above us. There were people everywhere. A woman from the Midwest stopped her family to point us out, too shy to come up to us. And yet, it was eerie. In the middle of rush hour, people were scurrying as I suppose New Yorkers always will. But it didn't look or feel like the New York we met in, even with a war raging around us. There were almost no dark faces, almost no brown or red or black or yellow faces. Forty-five million Americans died in that war, most of them in the camps. We must never forget that.

We sat for a while in the new Union Square, left the way the Nazis rebuilt it, another kind of memorial. A large circle with its statue of Beethoven in the middle, long rows of cherry trees radiating out from it in each direction. They were in blossom that morning, pink, windblown. The air was soft and a breeze coming in smelled of the sea. Arm in arm we headed back uptown. Izzy was very quiet, and went off to his study while I made dinner. After we ate, he read me the first draft of his last poem, "What Feeds Me," Izzy's imaginary account of his growing up reading Biblical stories about people like us, house full of the smell of his mother's chicken soup simmering on the stove for the Sabbath.

People of my generation remember Izzy the war hero. Their children remember the man who turned down the offer to be president so that he could shepherd the rebirth of Columbia University from under rubble. For twenty years, that was his passion, rebuilding and teaching. The poems of that era are optimistic, encouraging. But most of them were written at night at our kitchen table, wrung out of his sorrow, a man forcing himself to find meaning in life. He didn't think they were his best poems, but people of the next generation, who have to read them in school, who are sick of hearing their parents and grandparents talk about The War, still love those poems and continue to write me to say how inspiring they are. And we all know the words to "Together, Hand in Hand," set to music by the composer Leonard Bernstein, as the anthem for the United Nations, inscribed above the entry doors of the headquarters in Sydney.

Several months before he died, Izzy and I finished cataloging all his poems. They were written on scraps of paper, napkins, even rags that he had saved when paper became scarce during the war. And then the later poems, written on Columbia stationery, and the final poems, from the years of his retirement, when we traveled the United States, lecturing. There are 2,311 poems, some ten pages long, some only three lines. We worked for three years to organize them, sitting across from each other at the kitchen table. At night, we would go for long walks, often with our next door neighbor, Billie. We'd met Billie Holiday during the war. She'd escaped to the west when the Nazis began to bomb New York, and ended up leading a group of resistance fighters in Missouri. People who remember her as the Secretary of Cultural Affairs under President Kennedy often forget her earlier careers, as singer, as soldier.

One of our favorite places to walk to was Memorial Plaza where Wall Street used to be. We liked to sit in that open space, on one of the stone benches that ring the plaza. I remember one night in particular. It was sunset when we got there, coral turning to grey in the sky. Across from us, someone was sitting with a portable radio. When the wind carried it our way, we could catch bits and pieces of music. And then a cracking voice cried out, "President Roosevelt is dead."

I remember how we held each other. Feeling as if the mother of us all had died. To those who are younger, Eleanor Roosevelt is a part of history. But even though she had been out of office for years, she who had been there all through the war, her arched voice on a contraband radio the voice of our hope, was still the President to us.

I like to go back to sit on that bench. You can look all the way down the harbor, to the small domes on Ellis Island. Can look out across to the island where the Statue of Liberty once stood, where a new golden dome rises, the tomb of President Roosevelt. It seems fitting that she is buried there, not a statue of a mythological figure, but a monument to a real woman. Izzy's words, from the poem he read at her funeral, are carved around the bottom of the dome. He was proud of those words, and now that he is gone, they speak as much for his life as they do for hers. Read them here, and be with this man. Selfless, powerful, and tender, the work of Pink Izzy is a skyscraper of sound, a canon of peace, testimony to an era, and a portal to the transformed planet we all live on, its nations now blessedly united in one world government.

Avodah ∽

᪽ **Mincha** ᪽
Gazing out of a Window

Benjamin Zeiger, this year's Nobel Prize laureate in Literature, gave his first interview with the press in over forty years to Sybil Gruenberg of the *Warsaw Jewish Daily*, on June 30th, at the Center for Diaspora Studies, in a small reading room off of the main library, looking out on the Vistula River.

SYBIL GRUENBERG: You've often been compared to Marcel Proust, and to the American writer J.D. Salinger, also recluses. We're honored that you've chosen us for this interview. And yet, unlike Salinger, one aspect of your personal history is widely known. Shall we begin by talking about the fact that you come from a noted literary family.

BENJAMIN ZEIGER: [Laughing.] Even at my advanced age, I haven't left that legacy behind. Another man might be depressed. But unlike several of my sisters, I've been graced with a sense of humor about the fact that all of our lives, and ultimately my career, were shaped by Sholem Aleichem, who turned us into the characters in his stories about Tevye the Dairyman.

SG: In your Nobel acceptance speech you said that you've lived your life in a zone where fringe and center wed. Were you referring to that legacy in particular?

BZ: In part. My family comes from an obscure dorf in what used to be the Pale of Settlement, and we probably would all have remained there, or fled and been forgotten, were it not for my father's chance meeting with Sholem Rabinowitz, who the world knows as Sholem Aleichem. He and his family vacationed for several summers in our region, which is where he met my father, who was, just as the stories tell, the local dairyman.

SG: In what ways did your father resemble the Tevye that we all know?

BZ: Tevye the character and Mendel, my father, are near twins, closer than Esau and Jacob. To this day, when I go back to the stories, I always cry. They bring Papa back to life. Like the Tevye of literature, my father was constantly invoking Torah and Talmud. And just like Tevye he was a bumbling mangler of sacred texts, a great misadventurer, a Jewish

Sancho Panza and Don Quixote rolled into one. It's Rabinowitz' characterization of our mother Ruchel that was off. In the Tevye stories she comes across as a simple but pious, superstitious shrew. In fact she was tender, devoted, and a loyal and patient spouse to a man who could be trying on his best days. And, she was funny in her own right. Funnier than Papa. People assume my sense of humor came from him. It didn't.

SG: I understand that your father, unlike the fictional Tevye, ultimately made it to Palestine, and died there, in 1950.

BZ: Yes. My mother died in 1934, and the years that followed were difficult for all of us. Tevye had seven daughters. My parents had five. Just as the stories tell, my eldest sister defied convention and married for love, as did our next oldest sister, who, like her literary counterpart, followed a Marxist husband to Siberia, to Birobidzhan, where she eventually became the Minister of Education. My next sister married a non-Jew, which was painful for us to find written about. But what tore us apart was the death of my next sister, Bluma, a suicide. And when Rabinowitz' story came out soon after her tragic death, we were horrified that Papa's "old friend," as we always called him, would make public our private pain. For years Rabinowitz sent us money, which my father always sent back after Bluma's death. And he'd tear up and burn Rabinowitz' letters without reading them. An accidental meeting years later led to an awkward reconciliation and to several more stories about us, but for my father it was never the same between them. Rabinowitz was a charming and wonderful man. I remember as a little girl sitting on his lap while he told me stories, looking up at his big mustache, goatee, and hairless cheeks, so different from the long thick full beards of my father and uncles. But for all his charm, like many writers, he was a user of people, and an opportunist about his own career. He loved being called the Jewish Mark Twain. And worked just as hard in public to cultivate an image of himself that would endear him to the world as he worked at his desk.

SG: Might we say that some of your choices as a writer were made in opposition to the life of Sholem Aleichem?

BZ: Precisely. I've always felt that the work is about itself, not about its source.

SG: But might we also say that his life in many ways was an inspiration?

BZ: Yes.

Avodah :~

SB: Mr. Zeiger, as the first transgender recipient of a Nobel Prize, in your life and in your work, you have redefined our conventional ideas about gender and sexuality. In your speech in Stockholm you said that you accepted the award on behalf of all marginal peoples. Your first published novel, *Prize of Scalpel*, is about Martin Weissman, a small-town boy who transitions into a still-tormented girl. And in...

BZ: Remember, I set that book in 1933, just before Adolf Hitler was assassinated in Hamburg, when it looked like all of Europe's Jews were in danger. Critics have always assumed that Martin's despair is about his personal fate, but how could anyone in that time, Jew or non-Jew, with any kind of decency, not have listened to the rantings of Hitler and his cronies, without feeling a sense of hopeless despair? I shudder to think what might have happened if Hitler had lived, if the Weimar Republic hadn't survived. I was fortunate enough to have met and studied with Magnus Hirschfeld, the German Jew who first used the word "transgendered." When he founded the Scientific Humanitarian Committee in 1897, it was the first organization that supported the rights of people like me in the world, we modern-day eunuchs in search of ourselves.

SG: Did your parents know about your transition?

BZ: No. My mother died after I left home, but before my full transition, and I was estranged from my father before he died, as were several of my sisters. Not because of their marriages or because of my gender choice, but because we'd left the world of Orthodoxy, which was the only world he knew.

SG: You also dealt with a transgendered theme in *Burnt Letters*, when Emil Steinberg flees to Paris, to escape the confines of his family. It's been compared to the work of Franz Kafka...

BZ: Whom I met in Prague a year before he died. Yes. Some of my early work was influenced by his. And by his torment.

SG: In those years, I understand, you were living in Warsaw, passing as a man.

BZ: [Laughs.] To call it passing is to miss the reality of the situation. For myself, for other people like me, living on the edges of convention, although we may struggle, there's always an island of inner calm, a place that knows and says – this is me. Just as Adam was called by God to name all the animals, I always knew what my true name was, not the Breina my parents saw but the Benjamin I knew myself to be. The little girl who sat on a famous writer's lap was always a little boy to himself. My sisters were always shy, it not terrified, of Rabinowitz, especially when they were older and found out who he was. I, the youngest, was never afraid. I was pluckish and willful, and although this kind of gendered talk was considered suspect two or three decades ago, when gender was said to be a social creation, every little boy living inside a girl's body will affirm for you that boys and girls are not the same. If they were, no one but a total masochist or fool would endure repeated surgery and undergo lifelong hormone treatment.

SG: Literary critics and historians have called your father, or Sholem Aleichem's rendering of him, a portrait of the quintessential Jew of the past. The suffering, despair, the odd mixture of wisdom and absurdity, add up to what Freud called the Old Jew.

BZ: Although I've been for many years a recluse, my path has crossed that of several noted men. I spent a year in Vienna, in analysis with Dr. Freud. It was he who encouraged me to take the next step in my journey of self-creation.

SG: But...

BZ: I'm sidestepping your question. I don't want to become an icon for the New Jew. I don't want to be an icon for anything. Ours is an anti-iconic tradition. You ought to know that. We are forbidden to make images.

SG: Instead we just talk about them. Endlessly.

BZ: Touché, Madame. So, let us say that I *am* the icon for the New Jew. The big-nosed shuffling caricature that Hitler's cronies so loved to draw, has been replaced in the second half of the 20th century by this New Jew that we hear so much about. And I am its best representative, a surgically altered creature, parts divided, re-formed, and made new. Well, I don't buy it. This New Jew is old, he's Spinoza, she's Gluckl of Hameln. And that Old Jew, the scapegoat of hundreds of years of anti-Semitic rantings, was also an invention, no more real than Tevye and his daughters. A distorted mirror in a funhouse.

SG: Your sisters…

BZ: Are all dead.

SG: But did they feel the same way that you do?

BZ: Tevye and his daughters were always a joke. We were real human beings. Tevye and his daughters were comic, tragi-comic. But my sister Dvora buried her husband, then went back to school to support her children, and became a social worker, in the Jewish slums of Warsaw. Bluma took her own life. Leah left us for the gentile world. And Rivkeh became a Minister of Education in Birobidzhan.

Avodah ∻

SG: Where she promoted the work of the very man who...

BZ: I know, I know. It's ironic, isn't it? Promoted the work of the very man we all loved – and resented. But as artificial as it is, the Jewish homeland in Siberia continues to uphold the works of the fine Yiddish writers of the past, while we in the West turn our backs on them and call ourselves modern. But Peretz was always my sister's favorite writer, not our old friend. And now that all of my sisters are all dead, their children and grandchildren are far enough removed from the past that the attention they get is always rewarding for them. And I am close enough to death that the past seems more real in some ways than the present. And now I can talk about our old friend as if he were just one more character, in someone else's novel.

SG: I understand that you never met Peretz, although your stories that take place in heaven seem to have been inspired by several of his?

BZ: I arrived in Warsaw in 1918, three years after his death. I'd completed my brief analysis with Freud, was living as a man although surgery didn't exist yet. But I decided it was time to return home, to the Yiddish-speaking world I was born in, to Warsaw, where a hundred Jewish presses and twelve Jewish daily papers shone like stars in their constellations, calling out to me. My struggle before that had been to understand who I was. The Vienna years clarified that, and it was time to get on with my life. My life has been Warsaw, the capital of the Jewish world in our time. The capital of Jewish scholarship and literature. I was drawn to it, like a moth. No. Enough death imagery. I turned toward Warsaw like a sunflower turns toward the afternoon sun, in adoration.

SG: Your first short story was published a year after you arrived here. How does that early work look to you now?

BZ: There are stories I like and stories I don't like. Now that I've been noticed by the world, my agent tells me several publishers have approached her with offers to bring out my collected works. The same publishers who barely kept in print the few they still made money from.

SG: Several years ago I interviewed German filmmaker Anne Frank, who's turned several of your stories into movies, as she's done with a number of other Jewish writers. I remember her saying that you're the only writer she's ever known who could go back to an unfinished story, take up with it mid-sentence, right where you left off, and finish it two decades later. Is this true?

BZ: [Smiling.] My favorite of the three films Frank made from stories of mine is *My Life in Pajamas*. It's taken from a story, "He Was a Very Smart Girl," which I began in 1938 or '39. I never finished it. In fact, I forgot all about it. It turned up in 1951, in an old file folder that I discovered when my wife and I were moving to a new apartment. And I did take up with it right where I left off. But that's the only time I've ever done that.

SG: I understand that you've only met Frank twice.

BZ: We speak on the phone from time to time.

SG: Your work has always been called cinematic.

BZ: From an early age I was captivated by motion pictures. It never occurred to me that I could make one, but I began to write the films I saw in my mind. Those were my very first stories.

SG: Your late wife Vera Schpilberg was a photographer. Did her work influence yours?

BZ: Greatly. There were several long stretches of time when we lived apart. She did much of her work in Palestine. Her work with the Bedouins is probably what she'll be remembered for. But Warsaw has been my home for all of my adult life. Even when we were apart, we were sharing our work with each other. She was a great fan of Martin Buber's, and she used to joke that our work was in a constant I-Thou conversation, even when we weren't. She'd take pictures of things that I was writing about, and I'd dream about places she was photographing.

SG: In *Moscow Calling*, your own most comic work, you created a world in which the telephone was invented long before it actually was, and you transcribed the intimate conversations that Anna Karenina and her lover Vronksy were having.

BZ: You're being very diplomatic. Vera was married when we met. She left her husband to be with me, just as Anna left her tedious husband, and yes, our conversations were the inspiration for that story. I've always admired Anna, a woman who defied convention, and I was always sorry that she killed herself. In the old days deviants always had to commit suicide, and I never liked that. Well, one evening Vera called me from Tel Aviv and we had a very painful conversation. After we hung up, I remember fuming at her, pacing back and forth in my study, deciding that it was time for us to get a divorce. I was reading, rereading, *Anna Karenina*, when she called. The volume sat spine up on my desk as I was pacing. Then the phone rang again. It was Vera, and the second conversation took us off in such an intimate direction that when we got off, as I sat with a cup of tea and turned back to Tolstoy, I had the inspiration for the story. If we'd had to depend upon letters, our marriage would have ended. But we had the phone to connect us, and if Anna had had a phone, she and Vronsky would have sorted things out.

SG: At this stage in your life, are there still things you're sorting out?

BZ: I have lived long enough to have had my marriage blessed by the Chief Rabbi of Poland, and to see my work lauded by the very Jewish papers, yours included, that used to pan it as mystical and nostalgic, or comic and post-modern. I never could figure out how it could be all of those things.

SG: What are we to make of your most widely read work, *The Five Books of Mona*?

BZ: *Mona* outshines my best book, *Eden on Fifty Shekels a Day*, but it's still a book I'm proud of. Obviously, it was inspired by James Joyce's *Ulysses*. Every writer in Europe, and every Jewish writer after the Great War, did their best to write their own *Ulysses*.

SG: Instead of Joyce's half-Jewish Leopold Bloom, you gave the world Morris Fishbein, a half Jewish, half Zulu office worker who is fired from his job in

Johannesburg when he starts going to work in women's clothing.

BZ: It's embarrassingly derivative. Now. At the time that it was published it was a big success. I still get letters from fans who've read it, from all over the world. Some of them I have to get translated. Chinese. Gujarati.

SG: Were you ever in South Africa?

BZ: My South Africa is like Kafka's Amerika. And what I'm most pleased with in the book is how Morris-become-Mona lives out every story in the Torah, just as Bloom lived out Odysseus' journey.

SG: But that's what the rabbis condemned it for.

BZ: Mockery and satire aren't the same thing. And no book, no work of art, comes from nowhere. Every story has its own fertile soil, and every outsider has to use the dirt of the past, the work of the past, to anchor its roots in. I was my father's child, and I used what I knew best, the Torah. Just as Joyce used what he knew best. Greek myths.

SG: There's a story about you meeting Joyce, in Paris.

BZ: It's apocryphal. I didn't go to Paris until several years after his death. People confuse it with the story about the only time that Joyce and Proust met. They had nothing to say to each other, I've heard. Two of the greatest writers of the century.

SG: Neither of whom won a Nobel.

BZ: But Virginia Woolf did. And she turned down *Ulysses* but published the first English translations of Freud's and my work.

SG: I've heard that you maintained a long correspondence with Woolf.

BZ: Wrong again. It was with her long-time partner Doris Lefkowitz, who was my wife's second cousin.

SG: I didn't know that.

BZ: Good.

SG: Flaubert said that he was Madame Bovary. Are you Mona?

BZ: I was fired from the Warsaw Jewish Library in 1924, when they found out about me.

SG: Is there comfort in winning this award?

BZ: I feel like Job. God took everything away from him, his possessions, his wife, his children. And then later he was given a new wife, new children, new possessions. Only, Job was grateful.

It was late in the afternoon. The sun was low in the sky. Zeiger turned to gaze out the window, out across the river. If he were an observant Jew he would be heading toward synagogue for the evening service. Instead, Zeiger sat motionless and remained silent until the sun had dropped behind the buildings on the horizon. Then he reached across the table and turned off my tape recorder.

•

Avodah :~

～: Ma'ariv :～
The Return of the Hebrew Bedouin

The following account was written by an Israeli colleague who wishes to remain anonymous. This is the first time that it's been translated.

During the summers of 1979, '80, and '81 I worked as the cook at a small archaeological dig in the Negev. It was my job to feed two or three archaeologists, their five or six assistants, who were generally students or sometimes volunteers, and the changing crew of Bedouins who were hired to help out when extra hands were required. All the archaeologists and their students were Israeli but most of the volunteers were American. As for the Bedouins, they appeared for work when assistance was needed, mysteriously, as if someone had phoned them out on their camels. Because I had spare time between meals, and because I was generous with food, by the end of our first season I had become friendly with one of them, a tall slender young man of twenty-five or so named Mustafa. We would sit out behind the eating tent talking in a mixture of the bits of Hebrew he'd picked up and the Arabic I learned from my Algerian-born grandmother.

When I returned for the second year I was glad that Mustafa showed up again. One day several weeks into the season an old man appeared on his camel who I'd never seen before. Mustafa told me that he was an Ohadi. That was a clan I'd never heard of, but I sensed some reluctance on his part to say more, so I didn't ask Mustafa about him. The old man stayed one night, ate his own food, watered his camel, and was gone when I got up. Curious, I asked Mustafa who he was. "He is watching you," was all he said, then he changed the subject.

A week later the old man returned. I was nervous, knowing he was watching me. His face was dark and deeply lined, but he was vigorous, his eyes were clear, and he still had all of his teeth. I guessed him to be in his seventies. Knowing he hadn't come into the eating tent on his earlier visit, I brought a plate of food to him at his tent that night. In my best Arabic I offered it to him as my grandmother would have offered food to a guest in her house. He accepted, thanked me, said nothing else, so I returned to my tent.

The old man wasn't at breakfast or lunch, but he appeared with Mustafa, just after I'd cleaned up the lunch dishes. "He wants to talk to you," Mustafa said. "And remember, he is one of the Ohadi. One of your own people." I was startled by his remark, puzzled, and intrigued. Alone with him, the old man nodded at me and said, "You will come with me." He led me through a ravine behind the camp to the place where the Bedouin pitched their tents and kept their camels. He went into his tent, returned with a small carpet, which he rolled out and invited me to join him.

"I have been waiting for you. I instructed Mustafa to tell you who I am. I am of the clan of Ohad," he said, not in Arabic, but in a strangely accented Hebrew, unlike anything that I had ever heard before, at times difficult to understand. The situation felt both mystical and ridiculous. The child of a mixed marriage, my mother's family Algerian, my father's family Polish, I grew up in Tel Aviv with no religion except what I observed in the homes of my grandparents. There was a time in my twenties when I read a little Kabbalah, some Buddhist scriptures, and studied yoga with a teacher my sister found in Jaffa, but none of that penetrated as deeply as the words of that old man.

He was staring at me with eyes so dark that iris and pupil were the same. I felt like I was being tested. If I said the right thing he would continue. If I said the wrong thing he would leave and never return to our camp. I didn't have a bar mitzvah, but I felt in that moment as if I were on the verge of entering manhood. My brain was empty of reason and yet crowded with conflicting voices. Without thinking I blurted out the loudest words in my head. Addressing him as my grandmother taught me to address all older men, I said, "Grandfather, you honor me. I am your servant." He smiled, the first smile of his that I had seen. "And I am *your* servant," he said, with a slight nod.

Relieved, I smiled back. "Grandfather, please tell me why you have been watching this young man?" He glanced up at the sky and then looked back at me. "Your friend Mustafa told me that you are a good man, a friend of the desert people, and like myself, a Hebrew." I remembered that there had once been tribes of nomadic Jews who wandered between Yemen, Arabia, and Palestine, but I thought that they had vanished hundreds of years ago. So I said that to him, and just as he had smiled for the first time, he laughed for the first time, a rich and deep laugh. "You do not understand," he said. I looked down, embarrassed. "No, I don't understand," I said, "and I want to. But I have to go back to work. Will you meet with me after dinner?" The old man nodded and said he would come to my tent when it was dark.

I had to force myself to cook and snapped at the two volunteers who were working with me. Cleaning up was almost impossible. It took all of my will power to not run back to the old man's tent. But finally everything was put away. I went back to my own tent, and waited in front on a small folding stool.

The stars in the desert are amazingly bright. My brother-in-law told me it's because of the lack of humidity in the air that they shine so clearly. I was staring up at the sky when I felt the old man standing beside me. I looked up at him. He looked down at me. In the soft glow from the lamp I could see peace and satisfaction on his deeply lined face. "Come," he said, and I followed him. We walked a short way from the camp and when he sat down on a small stone I sat across from him on the ground.

We sat in silence for a while, and then he said, "I am of the clan of Ohad. Have you heard of Ohad?" I said no. He inhaled deeply. As hot as it is by day in the desert, it can be equally cold at night. I wished I was wearing another layer, and envied him his robe. "Tell me your name," he asked, leaning close. I told him and he repeated it. Then he said to me, "I am Ezer the son of Zalaf, the son of Amoz, the son of Elon, a descendant of Ohad the son of Simeon, the son of Jacob, the son of Isaac, the son of Abraham our father." Although he hadn't recited them all, I sensed that he could have told me the names of every generation of his ancestors, all the way back to Abraham. A shiver ran though me, and then a reaction to it. I wondered if he were demented, or playing a joke on me. But when I looked at him in the moonlight, moon a little less than full, I could see on his face only one thing, sincerity. "Tell me about Ohad," I asked him.

"That is why I am here. To tell you, my son. Because you are a Hebrew, although your journey and the journey of your clan and tribe have been very different than ours." I thought he was talking about the centuries of exile in the Diaspora and the return to the land of Israel. I thought he was talking about my education and my life experiences. But then he began to chant to me, strange Hebrew words that soon illuminated everything.

> *The sons of Jacob went down into Egypt, in the days of the great famine. Joseph their brother was a great chief in Egypt, after his brothers had sold him into slavery, all of his brothers, including Simeon the son of Jacob, our father.*

Ezer intoned these words, his dark eyes narrowed down to slits. In the chill, beneath the stars, I knew that what he was telling me was ancient and I knew that he was repeating it just as you repeat a Torah portion, word for word. To the best of my ability I am putting down these words as I heard them.

> *Joseph was a great man in Egypt, the right hand to the*

king. Joseph and his sons prospered in Egypt. Jacob and all of his sons prospered in Egypt, when they went down during the great famine. But Jacob was an old man. Before he died he gathered about him his twelve sons. He blessed each one of them, in the name of El Shaddai. "Now it is time to leave the land of Egypt and go back to the wilderness. Bury me with my fathers in the cave that Abraham purchased from the Ephron the Hittite to bury Sarah in, the cave where my father and mother are buried, the cave where I buried Leah my wife."

What Jew doesn't know the story about Joseph and the descent into Egypt, the story that leads to the horrors of slavery and then to the triumph and liberation of the Exodus? Only I didn't remember the part about Jacob telling his sons to leave Egypt. And the next part was unfamiliar too.

After Jacob died his sons prepared his body in the fashion of the Egyptians. But they said to one another, "Egypt has been good to us. Why should we go back to wandering as our fathers did? We will stay in this land of plenty. We will prosper and be glad here." Of the twelve sons of Jacob, not a one of them wanted to leave Egypt. And of the fifty and one sons of Jacob's sons, only Ohad the son of Simeon inclined his ear toward the words of Jacob. He said to his brothers, "We must leave Egypt." And they said to him, "Egypt has been good to us." Then Ohad went to his father and his uncles. "We must leave Egypt." And his father and all of his uncles said to him, "Egypt has been very good to us." So Ohad alone of all the house of Jacob, he gathered his wife and his sons and his daughters and left the land of Egypt, to return to their wanderings, just as El Shaddai had instructed Jacob, Isaac, and Abraham.

Then he was silent and I sensed that he would not say anything else. Silent myself, my body was still but my mind was racing. "Is he telling me the truth? Is it possible that a group of Hebrews left Egypt before the others had been forced into slavery? And is it possible that some of their descendants still exist? And if they weren't there for the Exodus, then they weren't at Mount Sinai and didn't participate in anything that to me signifies being Jewish, even if I reject most of it."

"But how can you be a Jew," I asked Ezer, "without Moses and the giving of the Torah at Mount Sinai?" Again the old man laughed, as if I'd just said the funniest thing he ever heard. Pointing at me, he said, "I am *not* a Jew. You are a Jew, a son of the tribe of Judah. But I am a Simeonite, a son of the tribe of Simeon, of the clan of Ohad, the only clan to follow the instructions of our grandfather Jacob. And yet, both of us are Hebrews, sons of Abraham."

When he said that a wave of certainty washed through me. In every cell of my body I knew that he was speaking the truth. I wanted to scream and stop him. I wanted to run away. I wanted to wake up from that strange dream. I wanted to convince myself that he was crazy. And I trembled in ecstasy.

The old man sat in silence for a long time. Finally I looked up at him and asked, "Why me?" He smiled. "Down through the ages the elders of our clan have sought out people from your clans, to see if you are ready to hear the truth about our people. So I have been watching and waiting, and I asked our friends of Ishmael if they had seen a son of Judah and Levi who could hear. For twenty years I have watched and waited. Then your friend Mustafa came and said there was a man in this place. A good man. A friend of the desert people. A true son of Jacob. I knew when I saw you that he was right."

"But didn't God promise our people the land of Israel to live in? But you don't live there." Ezer spoke slowly. "That is what your book tells you. Our people remember otherwise. We live as Abraham lived, not in one place but wandering, always, in the wilderness." I knew that thousands of Bedouin lived out in the desert. I remembered from school that in the time of Mohammed there were tribes of Jewish Bedouin who he hoped would join him. But his story, his words, were almost more than I could absorb. Pardon my analogy, but the only time I'd ever felt that way was when a friend at a party in Tel Aviv told me that the handsome bearded man who'd been flirting with me all evening had been born a woman. My brain could not readily absorb that information and it couldn't absorb what Ezer was telling me either. Not without asking him lots of questions.

"Do you observe the Sabbath?" He said his people knew a lot about the Jews, and that the Sabbath was a holiday of the sons of Judah, but that Abraham did not celebrate it, nor Isaac, or Jacob, or his own clan. That seemed impossible. In my mind Shabbat is the quintessential Jewish experience and our greatest gift to the world, a day of rest. I asked him if the Ohadi had any holidays at all. He said they celebrated the new moon because it is something you can see on your own. For them it is a day of rest, and he said they have four festivals during the year, celebrated near the solstices and equinoxes.

The spring holiday was the start of their year. They called it the Festival of Beginning, for that was when El Shaddai instructed Abraham to leave his home. The summer holiday he called the Festival of the Messengers, for that was when three angels came to Abraham and Sarah to announce the forthcoming birth of Isaac. The autumn holiday he called the Festival of Brothers, for it honored Jacob's returned to Canaan with his wives and children and his reunion with his brother Esau. And their winter holiday was named the Festival of Machpelah, for it commemorated the burial of Sarah in the cave of Machpelah that Abraham had purchased. But he told me that they also called it the Festival of Stories, for in that season the families of his people would gather together to retell their ancestral tales.

Although I don't keep kosher myself, I know a lot about it, being a cook. I asked him if his people ate pork. "We do not. Nor do our brothers of Ishmael." I asked him about eating milk and meat together. "When the angels came to Abraham and Sarah to announce the birth of Isaac they served them curds and milk and a newly slaughtered calf. That remains our most sacred meal."

I asked him if he knew about the commandments that God gave to Moses at Mount Sinai. He didn't answer me directly but said that when the other clans finally left Egypt the Ohadi were there to welcome them, only the other clans did not listen to the Ohadi. They had a new god. I asked if the Ohadi had any commandments. He said that their only laws were what El Shaddai told Abraham and Sarah when they left Ur. "Do not live within walls. Move when I call you. Find Me beneath the sky and the stars."

"Do you have a written book like we do, and the Muslims and Christians?" He said no, that all the stories of his people were told and retold from memory, but that he knew about our books. Since the time of Moses, he said, his people had kept watch on my people, so they knew our ways, however strange they seemed. I tried to imagine that, the Ohadi watching us for three thousand years, watching us and yet remaining apart.

The last question I asked him was if his people were also waiting for the messiah, as we have been. He laughed again. "We all stand equally before El Shaddai. Why do we need to be redeemed in days to come, when everything that El Shaddai created is here for us now, and when El Shaddai feeds us so well of His goodness?"

Ezer stopped speaking. I was shivering, chilled to the bone, but I hadn't noticed until then. He sighed and I felt a shift, as when a curtain falls at the end of a play. He asked me not to tell anyone what he had told me for twenty years. He asked me to live with his story until it had become a part of me. Then he thanked me. He said he had been waiting for me and he was glad that I had come. "One day, perhaps, the clans of Judah and Levi will be able to remember their true inheritance, their true faith." He stood, easily for a man his age. I stood. I knew he was about to go, but I realized, with great fear, that there was one more question I wanted to ask him, a question about my life that I had struggled with.

I tried to force out words, but they did not come. "I'll ask him tomorrow," I said to myself. Then he stepped closer, right up to my face. He put his large gnarled hands on my face, leaned close, and before I had a chance to stop him, he kissed me, on the lips. For an instant I was filled with disgust and rage. But the kiss became tender, our tongues slipping together like two merging streams. Then he pulled away, bowed, turned, and walked back to his tent. I turned and walked back to mine, feeling lost, confused, healed, met, and blessed, all at the same time. My unspoken question answered, in such an unexpected way, as if he'd been able to read my mind. My question about those troubling verses in a Bible that his people do not possess.

It was two in the morning. I was exhausted, but instead of going right to sleep I took out the notebook I keep recipes in. In the back I wrote down the words he had chanted, which were seared in my brain. Then I fell into a deep sleep, only to be awakened by my alarm clock three hours later, to start breakfast. Waking in my familiar tent I didn't at first remember the events of the night before. Then it all came back in a rush. I leaped into my clothes and ran to the Bedouin camp. Ezer's tent was gone. His camel was gone. Mustafa was up and waiting for me. "Where did he go? There are so many things I want to ask him." He put a hand on my forearm, something he had never done before. "It was time for him to return to his people. He said that El Shaddai will tell you everything you need to know."

I wanted to run out into the desert, following Ezer's camel's tracks, which were already obliterated by the wind. Mustafa tightened his grip on my arm. "It is time to make the morning meal. You will not find him. And we will not speak of this again, my friend." It was the first time he had ever called me that. I was incapable of motion, so he turned me around and pushed me toward the eating tent. Again I had to force myself to work. The moment I was done cooking I ran to find Mustafa, but he too was gone, and he did not return for the rest of that season.

That night and in the days that followed I made notes about everything I could remember. I felt like a fool. There were so many things that I could and should have asked Ezer, but I didn't. In my own defense, I was feeling overwhelmed, and it hadn't occurred to me that he wouldn't be there in the morning, to talk to, to learn from.

After Mustafa left I asked one of the archaeologists if there was a Bible in the small camp library. She said there was, that it was a useful tool of the trade. I borrowed the well-worn text and skimmed through it, not having read it for many years. I was looking for one word, one name, "Ohad." In truth, I hoped that I wouldn't find it, so that I could dismiss everything that had happened to me, and go on with my life.

Avodah ≈

There are several genealogical lists in the Torah. The first one I came to is in *Genesis 46:10*. It gives the names of the Israelites who had gone down to Egypt. There was Jacob, his son Simeon, and then the names of Simeon's six sons. One of them was Ohad! Stunned, I continued to flip through the book, knowing there were other lists. Sure enough, in *Exodus 6:15*, I found a partial list of clans that included the lineage of Moses and his family. And again, there was Ohad!

That night I called my sister. After chatting for a while I asked to talk to her husband. Although he is no longer observant, he went to a yeshiva and knows a lot about the Bible. Jokingly I told him that spending all day around old things had given me an interest in the Torah, especially the genealogical lists of the twelve tribes. Lucky for me, he remembered two lists that I hadn't found yet. As soon as I hung up I grabbed the Bible. In *Numbers 26:12* I found a list of the clans, from a census Moses took in the wilderness. To my joy and terror, this list was almost identical to the ones in *Genesis* and *Exodus* – except for one difference. The first two lists, from before the time in Egypt, both listed six sons of Simeon whose descendants became the six clans in the tribe of Simeon. But in the census after the Exodus there were only five clans listed in the tribe of Simeon. And the missing clan was Ohad!

Amazed, I turned to *1 Chronicles* 4:24, where I found an account of the clans of Israel from the time of King David. It gives a slightly different list of clans in Simeon, but once again there are five clans, not six, and it's Ohad that's missing. Below you will find the four lists, book by book, and see the minor variations between them. "Jemuel" becomes "Nemuel," "Jachin" becomes "Jarib," and "Zohar" becomes "Zerah," but you can also see the major difference: Ohad vanishes! Check for yourself and you will see.

Genesis 46:10	Jemuel	Jamin	Ohad	Jachin	Zohar	Saul
Exodus 6:15	Jemuel	Jamin	Ohad	Jachin	Zohar	Saul
Numbers 1:22	Nemuel	Jamin		Jachin	Zerah	Saul
I Chron 4:24	Nemuel	Jamin		Jarib	Zerah	Saul

Then I remembered what Ezer had said about the meal that Abraham and Sarah prepared for the angels. I was certain that he was wrong about that. But I went back to *Genesis*, and sure enough, it was exactly what he said it had been, a non-kosher meal of curds and milk and a calf. Are these things proof of what he told me? Hardly. But they're the only proof I have.

I spent the winter back in Tel Aviv, living with my parents and working in their restaurant. They were puzzled to see me reading the Torah, but both sets of grandparents were delighted. My sister and her husband teased me about it. I wanted desperately to tell them what had happened, but I honored Ezer's request. I read everything I could find about the Bedouins, but there was no mention anywhere of a clan named Ohad or about any surviving Hebrew nomads. Sometimes I thought that I had gone crazy, and then I would go back and read Ezer's words again, in my little spiral notebook. And sometimes I felt blessed by what had happened, felt a spirit of benevolence spreading out above me, like the fronds of a date palm under the fierce desert sun. And instead of slipping out of the house late at night to walk to Independence Park in search of quick sex, I remembered the sudden deep closeness I felt when Ezer kissed me, and found myself wanting that. And when I found myself drawn to another man, a new waiter in the restaurant, for the first time, instead of shame, instead of turning away from him or pushing him away when he reached out to me, I felt joy and a sense of rightness, and cautiously reached out to him. The relationship didn't last long. I didn't know enough to stay in it. But being with Gad changed me, just as my brief time with Ezer had changed, me, to the core.

I was invited back to cook at the dig the following year. It was a small site and I knew that that would be the last season of digging there. I looked forward to seeing my friends on the crew again, but more than that I was looked forward to seeing Mustafa, and of course, I couldn't wait to see Ezer again and continue our conversations.

Mustafa was there the day that we arrived, his tent already set up. He took my hands as I stepped out of the jeep, and smiled at me. Usually a very hesitant man when he's around other Israelis, he led me away from everyone else, oblivious to my reaction or to theirs. When we were out of earshot he turned to me. "Ezer sends his greetings. He and his people have returned to the wilderness, and you will not see him, ever again." I was shocked. I'd returned with pages of questions to ask about his people, and brought several empty notebooks, a cassette recorder, and a dozen blank tapes.

Standing there, I felt like a fool. Sensing my grief, Mustafa embraced me. Then he pushed me away from him so that he could look at me. His gaze made me feel like I was having my picture taken, by a camera that could peer into my soul. "But Mustafa..." I began. He put a finger on my lips. Sternly, he looked deep into my eyes, folded his hands on his chest, bowed, and after I bowed to him, he turned away.

There was so much to do. The volunteers would be arriving in two days. I had my tent to put up, a kitchen to set up, and three archaeologists to cook for. It was dark when I got back to my tent. Alone, I took out the now worn notebook I had written in the summer before, but it was little comfort. The moon was slim that night so I took my gas lamp and walked back to the site where the Bedouins had set up their camp. I couldn't find the exact spot where Ezer's tent had been, so I wandered the area, mourning his absence, feeling his presence, thanking him for what he'd given me, and also feeling occasional flashes of anger at him for not having given me more. Curiously, although the Bedouins had all camped in that spot in the first and second seasons, when a group of them arrived a few days later, they set up camp in a different spot.

And now, twenty years have passed, twenty years that have changed how I think of myself, as a Jew, as a man, a gay man, and as a Hebrew. I live within walls for most of the year. But I've learned to feel Something, perhaps Ezer's El Shaddai, when I walk, sit in nature, and when I caress Yusuf my lover, a decade into our relationship. Increasingly I feel that Something surrounds and sustains us, when we look into each other's eyes, when we turn to each other in the morning to share our dreams. And I feel It whenever we stretch out beneath the stars, shining as they did that night when I was with Ezer. I promised him that I would not tell anyone his story for twenty years, although I don't know why and don't know why he chose me to tell it. But tell it I have. To you.

∴ **The End** ∴

Avodah ∴

Afterword

~: Rabbi Camille Shira Angel

and Rabbi Dev Noily :~

Afterword :~

"Some events do take place but are not true; others are, although they never occurred." Elie Weisel, *Legends of Our Time*, 1968

As the rabbi (Camille Angel) and as a member (Dev Noily) of San Francisco's Congregation Sha'ar Zahav, we get to keep company with a group of Jewish, Queerish artists and activists, who take risks for the sake of being true and bravely share their stories. As Weisel attests, the truth holds forth despite evidence otherwise. Andrew Ramer's audacity to tell the queer truth, to authenticate queer experience, and reflect queer desire in the corpus of Jewish literature with his juicy and delicious tales distinguishes him as a queer, Jewish literary hero. Evocative with his gorgeous words, prolific among his contemporaries (especially if you count his twenty-three yet to be published manuscripts), author and muse, Andrew has written his way into the vanguard of a movement. Yes, the queering construction and transformation of Judaism is well underway and our friend Andrew Ramer is at the forefront of the parade.

Andrew the magnificent: storyteller, *magid*, healer, shaman, textual archeologist, creator of fantasy and ecstasy,

Andrew is a fount of hope and healing for readers, Jewish and non-Jewish, Queer and straightforward, across the aging continuum.

With *Queering the Text*, Andrew's life-giving contribution generously seeds the field of sacred literature and serves the religious purpose of repair, *tikun hanefesh*, the repair of the soul, and *tikun olam*, repair of the world. To get to know Andrew Ramer in these pages is a privilege. To get to know him, as we have, in our shared holy community is a rare gift.

Over the years, we have watched and collaborated with Andrew as he takes off his shoes and goes wading into the sea of Torah, the water rising up to his ankles, his knees, his waist, his neck and sometimes, over his head. He delights, splashes, plays and, at times, fights for his life against the rip tides pulling him out to sea. With his open heart and his wide smile, Andrew has brought us all along with him, until we're all soaking wet with Torah.

As part of the creation of our new *Siddur Sha'ar Zahav*, Andrew led workshops where our congregants could dive deeply into our liturgy and their own hearts, writing new prayers that fuse our ancestors' ancient intentions with our own lived truth.

Working with our bar and bat mitzvah students as they prepare to teach Torah to our community, Andrew is both tour guide and midwife. He leads and accompanies our young people as they immerse themselves in Torah, and emerge with insights about both themselves and the holy tradition they are taking into their hands. Andrew reads these young people with the same respect, clarity and probing that he brings to his reading of sacred text,

Afterword ∾

honoring the holiness in the soul of his students, as well as in the traditions he's transmitting.

Andrew's artistry as a writer and a teacher are precious gifts to those who take the canon of biblical, rabbinic and post-rabbinic texts seriously. Like Rabbi Ben Bag Bag of *Pirkei Avot*'s saying about the *Torah*, "Turn it and turn it, for everything is in it," Andrew turns and maneuvers the text with care and precision and behold, we are able to see ourselves at once retrospectively and anew.

This is Andrew's offering: he steps with his whole body into the space where our received tradition meets our living moment, and he refuses to let either be diminished, compromised or sacrificed. This is a space of abundant love and light, and all of us who enter it feel blessed to be here.

Andrew's Queer Jewish Hermeneutic/gaze is an act of spiritual resistance. He disrupts the 'there are no gays, lesbians, bisexuals, transgender people in our sacred texts' assumption by reclaiming excluded figures and voices, and helps us color in our queer ancestry by bringing untold stories into the public domain.

In 1986 Judith Plaskow erased the question of whether women's voices could be heard from our Jewish past with her opus, *Standing Again at Sinai: Judaism From a Feminist Perspective*: "If we begin with the assumption that Judaism is constituted by women and men, then we must be open to finding Torah far outside the traditional canon." In just as liberating a move, Andrew Ramer articulates *our* queer assumption that Judaism has been constructed by human beings with homoerotic desires as well as heterosexual desires, across a continuum of gender identities. Now, we are receiving a new *kabalah*: holy texts, sensual texts, texts that help us voice the sublime mystery of love, of open desire, of passion. Love stories that have been previously unknown to us come alive as Andrew creates and names beloved friends.

The realness that Andrew describes with his *midrashim* gives us new windows into our past and our future. We feel less alone as Jews with our queer desires. Andrew's stories provide us with company, even elders. We can identify with his characters and our associative reveries flow. Associative reverie is an experience that Abraham Joshua Heschel describes as "the imaginative projection of our consciousness into the meaning of the words" [*Quest for God*, p. 28].

From verses overlooked or misunderstood until now, Andrew provides us with a sense of belonging. Now we can find ourselves unequivocally at home in the history of our people – in the pages of our *siddur*, in the *midrashim* that amplify our texts. There can no longer be any doubt that we were there, we are here and we will continue to take part in the transmission of Torah. Andrew's project animates us to join in reclaiming our associative memories and writing them into life.

Andrew writes and reveals an essential queer companion commentary. If as Plaskow writes, "torah is a partial record of the Jewish people ... torah testifies to moments of profound experience, illumination and also mystery, when the curtain was pulled back from the endless chain of historical circumstance and some underlying meaning and presence were traced and read from the events of Jewish history," then, we experience Ramer's work as revelation, progressive and prophetic. Ramer uses the *midrashic* process, which Jews have traditionally used to broaden the

Afterword ~

possibilities of interpretation and meaning, to once and for all erase our queer erasure/invisibility in Jewish texts ancient, medieval and contemporary.

Christian, feminist theologian Rosemary Ruether said the "critical principle of feminist theology is the affirmation of a promotion of the full humanity of women. Whatever denies, diminishes, or distorts the full humanity of women is, therefore, to be appraised as not redemptive" [*Feminist Interpretation of the Bible*, 1985, p. 115]. Andrew's stories return full humanity to queerfolk and therefore to all of us. His queering of traditional Jewish ritual and liturgy is an act of redemption.

Transmitting Jewish and queer values, Andrew emboldens his listeners and readers to take a new approach in fulfilling the *mitzvah* to be fruitful and multiply. Andrew impregnates our received tradition by historical reconstruction and ignites students to join him in this creative and redemptive project.

We read in the Talmud about Rabbi Eleazar ben Azariah when he became the head of the *Beit Midrash* (House of Study). His predecessor, Rabban Gamliel, had restricted access to the *Beit Midrash*, and Rabbi Eleazar ben Azariah's first decree was to remove the doorkeeper and grant permission to everyone who wanted to learn to come in. On that day, hundreds of seats had to be added to the *Beit Midrash* in order to accommodate all those who wanted to learn Torah (Bavli Berachot 28a).

Andrew's queer *midrash* throws open the doors, and invites us all in to learn Torah with, and from, one another. And, seated comfortably at the table, we're called on to keep the doors open for whoever may feel, as we once did, that there is no place for them in the *Beit Midrash*.

Our hope for these stories is that they are read and treasured by an infinite number of human beings now and in generations to come. May this be God's will.

Afterword :~

Acknowledgments

For thousands of years storytellers sat around a flickering fire, beneath the circling stars. Now we sit alone, inside, tapping away on plastic keys, our tribe at one remove, or several. This book exists because of my scattered tribe. Thank you for your love, encouragement, and support:

Penina Adelman, Rabbi Camille Shira Angel, Jeanne Barrett, Julie Batz, Chris Beach, Zoë Beach, Alyson Belcher, Susan Berrin, Rachel Brodie, Michele Cavalier, Paul Cohen, Jay Davidson, Dan Dewberry, Maxine Einhorn, Mary Jane Eisenberg, Karen Erlichman, Janice Farrell, Sara Felder, Ari Lev Fornari, Michael Friedman, Bonnie Gintis, Eileen Gordon, Sarita Groiser, Andréa Guerra, Ava Guss, Anna Homler, Mark Horn, Pastor Sheri Hostetler, Irene Eber, Kevin Johnson, Mike Katz, Rose Katz, Jasminder Kaur, Samuel Kirschner, Rabbi Elliot Kukla, Amichai Lau-Lavie, Katherine Leahy, Jonathan Lerner, Shoshana Levenberg, Stefan Lynch, Joy Manesiotis, Lyssa Menard, Amelia Nahman, Rabbi Dev Noily, Jesse Noily, Gary Pelzner, John Perkins, Sheppard Powell, Carol Robin, Susan Sanford, Bill

Scala, Martha Clark Scala, Harvey Schwartz, David-Michael Searcy-Ramer, Don Shewey, Maggid Jhos Singer, Marty Spiegel, Michael Starkman, Max Strassfeld, Patanjali Venkatacharya, Rabbi Julia Watts-Belser, Julene Weaver, Marc Weinberger. My writing group, Lewis DeSimone, Erik Gleibermann, Patrick Letellier, Jim Van Buskirk. Richard Ramer for sharing this amazing journey. Steve Zipperstein for four decades of deepening conversation. And Irmgard Baum, every day.

Nancy Fay, Ian Philips, Greg Wharton, for supporting this book from the beginning. Rabbi Benay Lappe and Rabbi Eric Weiss, for your encouragement. Kevin Johnson, Jeffrey Shandler and Rabbi Jacob Staub for your close reading of the text. Steve Berman, Toby Johnson, and Bo Young for giving this book life. Alex Jeffers for turning mental essence into beautiful living substance. Michael Starkman for giving face to these stories. Andréa Guerra for capturing the moment before words. Daniel Chesir, for the loan of your beautiful megillah. Jay Michaelson for Zeek and Nehirim, Rabbi Camille Shira Angel for inspired teachings, Rabbi Dev Noily for guiding me back to stories, and the three of you for blessing this book with your words.

Everyone at Gay Spirit Visions, The Mountain, Hambidge, the Jewish Community Library of San Francisco, and First Mennonite. With deep gratitude to my Sha'ar Zahav family and my friends from Torah Study and Queer Torah Study.

And the angels who wake me with words in the middle of the night.

Credits

Publisher: Steve Berman
Front cover art and design: Michael Starkman
Photo of the author: Andréa Guerra
Text design and composition: Alex Jeffers

~: A Note from the Text Designer :~

I was (and remain) a writer long before I stumbled into text design. I'm protective of my own sentences and paragraphs when a designer gets her mitts on them. When I'm on the other side of the desk, I like to think I'll be as sensitive to the author's words.

Still, I don't often have a passionate emotional and intellectual love affair with a book I'm laying out. I never expected to have one with Andrew Ramer's *Queering the Text*.

For one thing, although I am *queer* and intimately involved with *text* on several fronts, I'm not Jewish. I don't think I quite knew what *midrashim* were before I first opened Andrew's word-processing file. I'm not a person of any sort of faith. Religion(s) can provide handy tropes and themes for use in my fiction but I don't have much time for deity(ies) in my life. Andrew hasn't quite convinced me otherwise, but how lovely if he could—how lovely if he could convince everybody in the world. For this deeply humane, deeply loving book—subversive, unpredictable, playful, wise, generous, mind-blowing, *queer*—imagines a world I would very much like to live in.

We had a little...I don't like to say argument, Andrew and I, during the design process. When he gently questioned some of my choices for the look and feel of his book, I got more defensive than I should. I had, in a way, forgotten he was the author. What I felt was that I had to protect this profound and dangerous book—not *my* vision of it but its own vision of itself. I think they call that "transference."

I'm not certain I actually *convinced* Andrew I'd made the correct decisions, but he listened, heard, considered, generously gave way. What I think is, when I spelled out the reasoning behind my choices, he understood I wasn't just picking random tools out of the designer's kit, trying approaches out merely for the sake of trying them, throwing things at the wall to see what stuck. (*I've* thought all those things about some designs.) I think he understood I was (am) entirely under the spell of his marvel of a book. I think he understood I was (am) grateful to him for writing it and thankful for the lucky constellation of chances that placed it, for a moment, in my hands. I think he understood how privileged I feel to be one of the people helping *Queering the Text* step out into the light, meet its readers (may they be legion!), and commence queering the world.

—*Alex Jeffers*, May 2010

ANDREW RAMER lives in the Imaginal Republic of San Francisco. He is a member of Congregation Sha'ar Zahav, where he facilitated weekly Torah Study for many years and co-facilitated Queer Torah Study. In addition to serving as a conversion mentor he coached twenty-six bat and bar mitzvah students writing their sermons, and was a major contributor to Sha'ar Zahav's newly published siddur.

Ramer's first and perhaps best book was a long out-of-print collection of short short stories, *little pictures*, which he also illustrated. He is the author of *Angel Answers, Revelations for a New Millennium*, the Lambda Literary Award Finalist *Two Flutes Playing*, and co-author of *The Spiritual Dimensions of Healing Addictions, Further Dimensions of Healing Addictions*, and the international best seller, *Ask Your Angels*. His short work appears in *Best Gay Erotica 1998, Best Gay Erotica 2001, Afterwards: Real Sex from Gay Men's Diaries, Quickies 3*, and two Jewish anthologies, *Kosher Meat*, and *Found Tribe*. His work appears online at *riverbabble, Doorknobs and BodyPaint*, and *Tattoo Highways*. Ramer writes a regular column on spiritual practice for the gay men's journal "White Crane" and an interview with him appears in Mark Thompson's book *Gay Soul*.

www.ingramcontent.com/pod-product-compliance
Lightning Source LLC
Chambersburg PA
CBHW050433240426
43661CB00055B/2371